ABDUCTION

The Story
of
Ellen Turner

Blenkins Press

ABDUCTION

The Story of Ellen Turner

by Kate M Atkinson

Published by Blenkins Press.
21 Langdale Close
High Lane
Stockport   SK6 8JG

November 2002

Printed by
Willow Printing
75/79 Back Cross Lane
Newton le Willows
Merseyside   WA12 9YE

ISBN: 0-9543896-0-3

Contents

Front Cover

Portrait which is thought to be of Ellen reproduced with the kind permission of Lancashire County Museum Service and the Trustees of Higher Mill Museum.

Portrait of Edward Gibbon Wakefield by an unknown artist reproduced by courtesy of the National Portrait Gallery, London.

Back Cover

Portrait of Thomas Legh of Lyme reproduced with the kind permission of the National Trust.

Lyme Hall, south front.

Bibliography

O'Connor, I.   Edward Gibbon Wakefield. The Man Himself.
                        Selwyn & Blount   1928

Bloonfield, P.   Edward Gibbon Wakefield. Builder of the British
                        Commonwealth.   Longmans   1961

Harrop, A. J.   The Amazing Career of Edward Gibbon
                        Wakefield   Allen & Unwin   1928

Booth, P. H. W.   From Medieval Park to Puritan Republic
                        Lancashire Local Studies   1963

Baines, E.   History & Gazeteer

Picton, J. A.   Memorials of Liverpool   Walmsley
                        1903

Whale, D. M.   Lost Villages of Liverpool   Stephenson & Sons
                        1984

Chandler   William Roscoe of Liverpool 1753-1831
                        Batsford   1953

Davies, S.   History of Macclesfield   Manchester
                        University Press   1961

Earwaker, J. P.   East Cheshire 1880

Earles, J.   Streets and Houses of Old Macclesfield
                        MTD Rigg Publications   1990

Aspin, C.   The Turners of Helmshore & Higher Mill
                        Higher Mill Museum Trust   1970

Abram, W. A.   History of Blackburn J. G. & J. Toulmin
                        1877

Miller, G. C.   Blackburn, the Evolution of a Cotton Town
                        Blackburn Town Council   1951

Sinclair, O.   Gretna Green. A Romantic History   Unwin
                        Hyman   1989

Margetson,S.   Journey by Stages   Cassell 1967

Gore's Directories

Pigot's Directories

The Trial of Edward Gibbon Wakefield, William Wakefield & Frances
Wakefield Indicted with one Edward Thevenot, a Servant, for
Conspiracy and for the Abduction of Miss Ellen Turner... John Murray
                        1827

The Roscoe Papers   (Liverpool Record Office)

Acknowledgements

During the sixteen years I have been researching and talking about writing Ellen's story, I have been assisted and encouraged by many people throughout the North West. Libraries in Blackburn, Macclesfield, Manchester, Kendal, Carlisle and the British Library Newspaper Library have always been most helpful. The Record Offices in Liverpool, Greater Manchester and Chester have provided me with much of my information. I am particularly indebted to Susan Nicholson from the Field Archaeology Section at Liverpool. Thanks to the assistance of their staff, I have been able to access the archives and collections at the Museum of Lancashire Life in Preston, Higher Mill Museum at Helmshore and Lancaster Castle.

Commercial organisations have also been generous with their time. The help of the staff at Shrigley Hall Hotel and Valerie Phillips at Gretna Hall Blacksmith's Shop has been much appreciated.

North Cheshire Family History Society and numerous local history societies have answered my many queries. Fellow researchers, in particular Barbara Riding in Blackburn, have provided essential nuggets of local information.

I am hugely indebted to Peter Neville and to my son, Graham, for their technical expertise and time in processing most of the illustrations. In the last few weeks the help of Carol Christian, Margaret Herbert and Elly Chave has been invaluable. My ex-colleagues at Lyme and my family and friends have tolerated my obsession with Ellen's story with amazing good grace and have provided constant support.

I would never have completed the story without the help of the people I have mentioned - and many more. Inevitably it will contain some mistakes for which I take full responsibility.

The Announcement

Saturday, March 11th, 1826 had been a long day for William Turner. His business affairs had led him to spend the previous few days in London and the journey back to his country seat, Shrigley Park near Macclesfield, had taken most of the day. Travelling by carriage was decidedly uncomfortable, so no doubt he was glad to have reached Shrigley and to relax with his copy of "The Times".

His wife, Jane, a semi-invalid, was at home with his sister Ellen, Mrs Henry Critchley. It had been a busy day, for the new house was abuzz with all the builders and decorators busily trying to complete their work ready for the public breakfast in three weeks' time. This was to mark the start of Turner's year as High Sheriff of Cheshire.

Their one surviving child, Ellen, the richest heiress in Cheshire, had just celebrated her fifteenth birthday. She was to miss the breakfast and the start of the ceremonial as, a few days before his visit to London, Turner had taken her back to the exclusive boarding school run by four sisters, Phoebe, Elizabeth, Margaret and Ann Daulby.

"The Times" was then made up of a mere four pages. Most of it was taken up with the national news of the day and with the reports from both Houses of Parliament. But on page three there was the announcement of a marriage which sent William and Jane Turner's world reeling -

> *"On the 8th inst, Edward Gibbon Wakefield, Esq., to Ellen, only daughter of W. Turner, Esq., of Shrigley Park in the County of Chester."*[1]

Their precious daughter married! How? She was at school. She was only fifteen. The Turners knew of no Edward Gibbon Wakefield. Who was he? The marriage was on the 8th - Wednesday. It was now

---

[1] "The Times" 11 / 3 / 1826

Saturday evening. Where were the couple? What on earth was to be done?

Panic must have set in. Mrs Turner's health was precarious, the shock could well have killed her. It was fortunate that her sister-in-law was there to give her support, because William, the clear-thinking business man, took action that many of his contemporaries in similar circumstances would have rejected. He decided to risk a scandal and to institute a search for his daughter.

He was a kindly father and Ellen was important to him, but practically she was a mere pawn. The object at stake was the Turner family fortune. Ellen was heir to both William and his brother, Robert, his partner in the family business back in Blackburn. If this alleged marriage was not challenged, Ellen's inheritance would by law be Wakefield's, for in those days any money a married woman possessed automatically became the responsibility of her husband. If her father could prove in law that the marriage was illegal then the fortune would revert to the Turner family.

At least by going to law, Turner stood a slight chance of retaining the money and of choosing for Ellen a husband of whom he approved and thereby of selecting the heir to the family business and wealth. To be sure it would be difficult, not many men would be prepared to risk marriage with a "disgraced" woman. Moreover if he subjected this marriage to public scrutiny by challenging it, Ellen would certainly suffer disgrace and notoriety, however innocent she most certainly was.

Probably the Turners expected Wakefield to make contact with them fairly soon for there were two possible ways for him to gain control of Ellen's inheritance. One method was to wait until Turner died but that might prove too long a time to wait as Turner was only fifty. The other way was the more common at the time. A scheming fortune-hunter would marry an heiress and would gamble on her parents' unwillingness to subject their family to scandal. He would then proceed to ingratiate himself into the family. If this latter method was Wakefield's ploy, he would have to make contact with Turner.

So William Turner set himself the task of finding and recovering Ellen as quickly as possible and then of bringing Wakefield to justice. This was three years before Peel established the first police force to fight crime in London. Turner was forced to rely on his own and his friends' detective work and knowledge of the law. To his advantage he had contacts and influence over a wide area, built up over his years in business. His first act was to send a message to his agent and legal adviser, Thomas Grimsditch, whom he had left in London. He then summoned Henry Chritchley, his brother-in-law, and Robert Turner from Macclesfield. They needed to know how, when and by whom Ellen had been taken from school, so a relative was ordered to write to the Daulbys. They also had to find out just who Edward Gibbon Wakefield was and where he was likely to be.

The hunt for the abductor and his supposed bride was under way. What followed was to be reported across the length and breadth of the nation. Wakefield became the most reviled malefactor in the kingdom. The sheer effrontery of the man seems incredible these days, but his story and that of Ellen, his unwitting victim, is true. It actually happened and it changed the course of many lives.

Mrs Margaret Daulby   Pencil drawing by T. Hargreaves
From "Memorials of Liverpool" by J A Picton. 1903 G G Walmsley
Reproduced by kind permission of Liverpool City Council   (Record Office)

Ellen is Snatched

The abduction had been executed so skilfully that no-one at the school realised anything was amiss for a whole five days. The very select band of young ladies from wealthy families continued with their lessons from the four sisters and visiting tutors. The Daulby family was superbly well connected. Their father Daniel was a poet who married Margaret, sister of William Roscoe, the historian, author and poet to whom a growing band of refugees in Liverpool looked for patronage. Ellen was taught Italian by the young Anthony Panizzi who later became the highly respected chief librarian of the British Museum.

Daniel and Margaret had lived with their family in the Lake District where they adopted the fashionable pastoral life, milking their cows and cheesemaking. When Daniel died, Margaret returned to Liverpool and with her daughters established a school from which they could all earn a living. The business continued to flourish, even after the death of Mrs Daulby, thanks to their connections in the town. It had moved fairly frequently but at the time of Ellen's abduction it was in a prime position at Fair View, a corner site at the junction of High Park Road and South Street in rural Toxteth. Most people today inevitably link Toxteth with horrific riots, drugs and police no-go zones. In 1826 it really was quite pastoral. It had been a deer park separated from its neighbour Liverpool by a stretch of countryside. Building of a few houses and roads to service them had just started on the land which previously had been farmed. Nearby on the banks of the Mersey there were two well known beauty spots, Dickensons Dingle and Knots Hole. A gentle stroll further along the riverside was Otters Pool. Thus the school was ideally placed to attract parents who wished their daughters to be prepared for their futures as wives and mothers in great houses by the most genteel and well thought of tutors.

The first inkling the sisters had that Ellen had been unlawfully taken from their care, was when a letter from Ellen's cousin Margaret

Miss Daulby   Pencil drawing by T. Hargreaves
From "Memorials of Liverpool" by J A Picton. 1903 G G Walmsley
Reproduced by kind permission of Liverpool City Council   (Record Office)

Miss Daulby   Pencil drawing by T. Hargreaves
From "Memorials of Liverpool" by J A Picton. 1903 G G Walmsley
Reproduced by kind permission of Liverpool City Council   (Record Office)

came on the Sunday. She explained that her mother and Dr Davies, the former vicar at Pott Shrigley had discussed the situation, that the family were greatly distressed and that they wished to see one of the sisters immediately. It was probably Elizabeth, though this is not certain, who set off for Shrigley with William Roscoe. Presumably they had looked to him for support in the face of such a catastrophe. The pair reached Macclesfield where they stopped the night, before presenting themselves to Ellen's father on the Monday morning, six days after the abduction, to explain what had happened.

Quite simply they had been hoaxed. Early on the previous Tuesday morning their serving girl had answered the bell. On opening the front door she found a green barouche - a four person carriage with a seat for the driver at the front - in the street and a French servant on the doorstep with a message for the Misses Daulby. He was taken inside and the sisters were summoned. He complained of a headache after travelling all night so he was given a brandy while the letter he had brought was read and endorsed to show it had been received. The letter completely deceived the schoolmistresses. It purported to come from Dr Ainsworth, Mrs Turner's doctor and read,

"SHRIGLEY,

Monday night, half-past twelve,

MADAM,- I write to you by the desire of Mrs. Turner, of Shrigley, who has been seized with a sudden and dangerous attack of paralysis. Mr. Turner is, unfortunately, from home, but has been sent for, and Mrs. Turner wishes to see her daughter immediately. A steady servant will take this letter and my carriage to you to fetch Miss Turner; and I beg that no time be lost in her departure, as, though I do not think Mrs. Turner is in immediate danger, it is possible she may soon become incapable of recognising anyone. Mrs. Turner particularly wishes that her daughter may not be informed of the extent of her danger, as, without this precaution, Miss Turner may be very anxious on the journey; and this house is so crowded, and in such confusion and alarm, that Mrs Turner does not wish anyone to accompany her daughter. The servant is instructed not to let the boys drive too fast, as Miss T. is rather fearful in a carriage. I am, madam, your obedient servant,

John Ainsworth, M.D.

The best thing to say to Miss T. is, that Mrs T. wishes to have her daughter home rather sooner, for the approaching removal to the new house; and the servant is instructed to give no other reason in case Miss Turner should ask any questions.

Mrs. Turner is very anxious that her daughter should not be frightened, and trusts to your judgment to prevent it; she also desires me to add that

her sister, or niece, or myself, should they continue unable, will not fail to write to you by post."[1]

Ellen was summoned but she recognised neither the servant nor the carriage. The servant said his name was Thevenot, that he had been a butler to Mr Legh of Lyme Park, the neighbouring property to Shrigley and that Mr Turner had taken him on for the new house. Mr Turner had gone to London in his own carriage so Dr Ainsworth had sent his carriage and Dr Hull, who was Mrs Turner's usual doctor, would meet Ellen at Manchester. This plausible tale was accepted and Ellen took her place in the barouche with Thevenot outside on the box next to the driver of the horses. So Ellen's abduction was accomplished and the Daulbys were none the wiser.

The Turners now knew how Ellen and her teachers had been deceived but Miss Daulby's story was no help in tracing Ellen. She had left Toxteth in a green barouche with a mysterious Frenchman and was married the next day at Gretna Green. And that was a whole five days ago. Where was she now? The detective work continued apace.

Meanwhile Miss Daulby and her uncle returned to Toxteth.

---

[1] "Lancaster Gazette" 24 / 3 / 1827

Tracking Wakefield Down

The first real clue came in the form of a letter written from Carlisle just after the marriage, by Wakefield, to his new father-in-law. The letter had reached Shrigley on the Saturday but such was the confusion caused by the announcement that it lay unread until the next day. In it Wakefield said that the blame was all his and that Ellen was an innocent and excellent child! He was writing to take all the odium and to relieve Mr Turner of all anxiety. Miss Turner was in good health, but her letter to her parents, which he enclosed, had been dictated by him *"for she, poor girl, knew not what to write."*[1] And this was supposed to convince the Turners that all was well! But, in the hunt for the couple, the vital clue was that Wakefield had given his address - Paris, Rue de la Papinnaire, No 66.

There was another source of information close at hand in Dr Davies, but at no time in any of the reports is it mentioned that he gave the Turners any assistance apart from that first discussion with Ellen's aunt. The highly respected Dr Davies, who was also the Headmaster of Macclesfield Grammar School, must have been totally baffled for he not only knew Edward Gibbon Wakefield, but only a fortnight before, the abductor had been a guest in his own home. Surely he must have told the Turners what he knew of the Wakefields in order to reunite them with their daughter, even if he did not immediately apportion any blame. Maybe he thought Ellen could well have known Wakefield and was a willing, if misguided, accomplice. But this is mere speculation, there is no evidence to prove the theory. So let us leave Dr Davies' connection for the moment and go on to what is certain.

In London, Turner's agent and lawyer Thomas Grimsditch had also read the announcement in "The Times" and was taken aback. He was not just an agent but was a powerful man in his own right. His

---

[1] "Macclesfield Courier" 27 / 5 / 1826

practice in Macclesfield looked after three local estates, Turner's in Shrigley, Thomas Legh's at Lyme and that of the Leghs of Adlington where he became a dominant figure during a difficult time for the owners. He was also the proprietor of the local paper, the "Macclesfield Courier". From 1837 to 1847 he served as one of the town's M.Ps and he was its mayor in 1860.

In the early hours of Tuesday morning he heard of the abduction, presumably when he was joined in London by Ellen's father, her uncle and Robert Turner[2] and they set about tracing Wakefield. It seems that at this stage Grimsditch did not know that he, like Dr Davies, had met Wakefield a couple of weeks before. The lead they appear to have concentrated on was the announcement in the paper. They discovered that it had been placed by a clerk, a Mr Edwards, who worked for a land agent called Edward Wakefield.

This Edward, the prospective parliamentary candidate for Reading, lived in Palace Yard at Westminster and it just so happened that it was also home to a widow called Mrs Pattle. She was the mother-in-law of Edward Gibbon Wakefield who had abducted her heiress daughter, a ward of court, in 1816, just ten years before he tried to do the same to Ellen! No wonder the abduction had gone so smoothly - practice makes perfect!

Turner could have no doubts, Wakefield must have taken his daughter to France. But this posed another problem, for there was no extradition treaty, added to which, they could not yet prove the marriage with Ellen was illegal. They could however accuse him of taking away a minor without her father's consent and an arrest warrant was speedily procured for this offence. They also took the precaution of obtaining a letter from Canning at the Foreign Office to Lord Granville, the Ambassador in France, in case they needed his help.

By Wednesday everything was in place ready for action and Critchley, Robert Turner, Grimsditch, a Bow Street runner called Ellis and a lawyer, Mr Wallford, took the steam packet from Dover. There was one more significant passenger on that boat, the Honourable Algernon Percy, for whom Wakefield had worked when Percy was the

---

[2] Robert Turner's relationship to Ellen is uncertain. She and others referred to him as her uncle but his known dates do not fit with any of the Roberts in the Turner family tree. He was certainly Henry Critchley's brother-in-law. Was the relationship between all the branches of this extended family so close that he was an "honorary" uncle?

under-secretary at the British Legation in Turin. Percy, of course, would have been privy to events at the Foreign Office from where the letter to the Ambassador in Paris had been obtained.

Reports of what happened when the boat docked at Calais in mid-afternoon vary. If we are to believe the more romantic version, while Ellen was strolling on the quayside, she spied her uncle Henry, threw herself into his arms and so was rescued. Ellen's evidence in court disproves this. According to her they were on the quayside from where she thought she recognised her uncle on the boat and then saw both her uncles when they had disembarked. Wakefield had told her that he did not want to meet them there, but they would go to their hotel where he would prefer the meeting to take place. Wakefield had then stayed in the hotel courtyard talking to Percy. He, of course, could have told Wakefield that the uncles had a Bow Street runner with them and that they had a letter from the Foreign Office. He remained nearby leaving Wakefield to face the music.

Meanwhile Grimsditch's first act was to go to the French police to request an officer to accompany them. They then went to the wrong hotel and were redirected to the Hotel Quillac. The ever confident Wakefield knew he could not be forcibly taken from France and was quite willing to meet the friends and relatives of the person he considered to be his lawful father-in-law. His charm and the wronged family's fear of scandal had worked once, why should it not succeed again?

They met Wakefield in the hotel courtyard. The situation could have become quite heated but Grimsditch seems to have been firm, calm and reasonable. Wakefield invited them to his room and when Ellis tried to go too, Grimsditch insisted he should remain outside - the Turner's very private business would not be transacted in front of a lowly Bow Street runner. He and Robert Turner confronted Wakefield and told him he would be prosecuted and that their lawyer's opinion was that the marriage was invalid. They quoted the letter from Canning which Wakefield told them he already knew about from Percy. Ellen's uncle Henry then came in and they all re-emphasised that proceedings would be taken against him.

Then Wakefield played his trump card. He confessed he had a daughter and that if any man tried to abduct her he would shoot him. But he considered that the marriage was legal and that Ellen was his lawful wife. At this Henry Critchley is reported to have said,

"I wonder how you can expect that we should enter into such terms. We must see her - you may have made some impression upon her."[3]

Wakefield agreed - he had nothing to lose. So Ellen was summoned from Mme Quillac's sitting room downstairs, entered the room and immediately flung her arms round her uncle Henry. Grimsditch and Wakefield left her with Critchley and Turner. And now Wakefield made a grave error. He admitted to Grimsditch that the marriage had not been consummated. For the Turner supporters that was their first bit of good news and they lost no time in taking full advantage of the admission. Grimsditch went back to Ellen and they left Wakefield kicking his heels outside for twenty minutes.

According to Critchley's evidence at the trial, during the time he had alone with Ellen, he had told her that the marriage was void. Her reply had been, "Thank God for it. It is the happiest intelligence that could be conveyed to me." We shall see later that Ellen was probably thinking of her father's situation at this point rather than the supposed marriage.

On being readmitted to his room Wakefield was told they were arresting him and taking Ellen back to her father. He had his answer ready - he was on the wrong side of the water for that. He continued to say that the marriage was valid whilst the others stated it was not. Eventually Ellen spoke, "I am not your wife. I never will go near you again - you have deceived me." By this time the poor girl was in quite a state and was clinging to her uncle. Wakefield replied, "You must acknowledge I have behaved to you as a gentleman." To which Ellen's response was, "Yes I do acknowledge that; but you have deceived me and I will never go near you again." They again pointed out that marriage by force or fraud was illegal.

Wakefield denied the force but said, "I do not justify my conduct," and referred again to his own daughter.

Critchley tried once more by quoting Sir Robert Birnie's advice that the marriage was illegal. The French policeman was called in and said that if the marriage was legal the law in France would not separate husband and wife. However Ellen stated that she was going with her uncle. Wakefield did not try to stop her. He knew it would not help his cause and he could still fight to prove the marriage's legality.

---

[3] "Macclesfield Courier" 27 / 5 / 1826 from which all the quotations on this page are taken.

Thus they prepared to take Ellen back to England to her anxious parents. But before leaving, Robert Turner made sure of the vital bit of evidence. Wakefield actually signed this statement which was later printed in the " Macclesfield Courier"[4]

"Calais, March 15th,1826

Sir,

At your request I hasten to repeat in writing the solemn assurance which I have just made to you, namely, that my marriage with your niece has never been consummated, and that since she has been with me, I have treated her most punctiliously only as my sister.

I know not how this declaration may affect the validity of my marriage, nor whether, in a legal point of view, it may be injurious to me; but I rejoice to be able to make it , hoping that it will prove some comfort to Mr and Mrs Turner in the midst of their distress.

Their daughter will state to them how exactly it is true.

I have the honour to be, Sir,

Your most obedient humble servant,

Edwd G Wakefield

Robert Turner,Esq & &

15th March 1826

This letter was delivered by Mr Wakefield to Mr R Turner at Quillacq's Hotel, Calais, in my presence.

Tho Grimsditch."

So the rescue was accomplished and Ellen was on her way home, but there was to be a long battle ahead before she was free of Edward Gibbon Wakefield. He made sure the legal process dragged on and on for over a year.

And how the press loved it! Every salacious detail was gleefully revealed to their gossip-hungry readers. All Ellen and her family could do was to try to retain a dignified silence.

---

[4] "Macclesfield Courier" 31 / 3 / 1827

Wakefield and his Family

To make sense of the story we must now leave Ellen and concentrate on Wakefield and his motives. Many books have been written about him, some extolling his virtues as a pioneer of the Commonwealth, another on a more personal level by one of his descendants, Irma O'Connor.[1] What they reveal is an extraordinary life from infancy to old age.

Edward Gibbon Wakefield was born in 1796, the second child in a family of nine children. His father, a dreamer, had lost a fortune in a business failure. His grandmother, Priscilla, was a practical lady. She had initiated the savings bank movement and was aunt to Elizabeth Fry, the prison visitor and reformer.

O'Connor quotes from Priscilla's diary which reveals the grandmother's despair over the lives of her son and grandson. In 1799 she was wishing that her son had fewer wild plans and was more interested in his parental duties. It was not to be, for two years later he was taking an avid interest in prisons and workhouses rather than exerting some control over his offspring. She disapproved of her grandson's upbringing but expressed the hope that she might be able to influence him despite the fact that all the freedom he was given at home made *"orderly restraint"* very difficult. In 1807 young Edward was sent to Westminster School and his grandmother wrote that when he was obstinately set on something evil she was terrified, but that if he set his mind on doing something good he would be showing *"noble firmness"*. The future abductor was then all of eleven! He lasted three years at Westminster and refused to go back. So it was on to the High School in Edinburgh from where his father had to remove him a year later in disgrace. Yet another opening was tried in 1813 when he was admitted to Gray's Inn.

---

[1] "Edward Gibbon Wakefield The Man Himself" Irma O'Connor. Selwyn & Blount 1928

At eighteen he became secretary to the Honourable William Hill, later Lord Berwick, who was envoy at the court of Turin. He returned to London with Mr Hill in 1816 and fell in love with his employer's ward, the sixteen year old Eliza Pattle. Her father had been a wealthy merchant and she was then living, as a ward in Chancery, with her mother and two uncles at Tunbridge Wells. The impecunious Wakefield knew he would not be regarded as a suitable husband for the heiress and so devised an ingenious plan to elope with her. Firstly he deliberately tried to ingratiate himself with Eliza's uncles by joining them in their favourite sport, cock-fighting. Having gained their confidence he took action. Two coaches were hired, in one Wakefield and Eliza fled north, the other was the decoy and went south, hotly pursued by the uncles. By way of relations in Ipswich, the couple went to Edinburgh where they were married.

The marriage was announced in London in the "Courier" on the second of August -

"Lately, in the City of Edinburgh, Edward Gibbon Wakefield Esq., eldest son of Edward Wakefield, Esq of Pall Mall, to Eliza Anne, the only child of the late Thomas Charles Pattle, Esq, of Canton."

It took just a week, with Mr Hill's support, for Wakefield to win over his mother-in-law and to save himself from the wrath of the Lord Chancellor, who could have been asked to prosecute Wakefield for marrying a ward of the Court of Chancery without the necessary permission. The couple went through another marriage ceremony in London and so Wakefield found himself with a wife and her annual income of £2,000 plus the expectation that it would double on his mother-in-law's death. The rest of his life seemed rosy. For what more could a young man wish!

The couple went to live in Genoa where Wakefield became secretary to Percy at the legation in Turin. Their first child, Susan Priscilla, known as Nina, was born in 1817. Their second child, Edward Jerningham, was born in June 1820 but Eliza died ten days later aged only twenty. The twenty four year old widower was left to bring up two babies. By then he had moved to the Embassy in Paris and employed a French governess for the children. Eliza's tragic death did nothing to alter his character. He remained a dreamer just like his father - better things were always just around the corner.

At his house he surrounded himself with a group of his family and friends who seem to have encouraged him in his extravagant ideas.

Wakefield

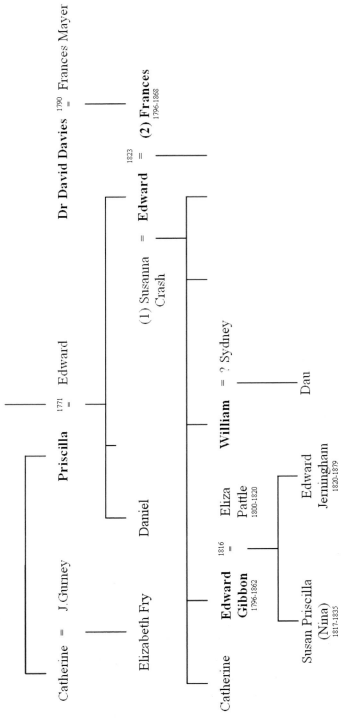

Catherine = J.Gurney

Priscilla ¹⁷⁷¹ = Edward   Dr David Davies ¹⁷⁹⁰ = Frances Mayer

Elizabeth Fry   Daniel

(1) Susanna = **Edward** ¹⁸²³ = **(2) Frances**
     Crash   1796-1868

William = ? Sydney

Dau

Catherine

Edward ¹⁸¹⁶ = Eliza
Gibbon   Pattle
1796-1862   1800-1820

Susan Priscilla   Edward
(Nina)   Jerningham
1817-1835   1820-1879

His brother William was a close companion and seemingly under the spell of his elder brother, though he appeared less rash. It was suggested a lot later in Edward Gibbon Wakefield's life that he used his piercing eyes to practise hypnosis. However he did it, he succeeded in building a little coterie around himself which the members referred to as the "first society in Europe".

The turning point for them all came when Edward Wakefield senior remarried, at the Embassy in Paris, in August, 1823. His bride was the much younger Frances Davies whose father, the Reverend Doctor Davies, the Headmaster of Macclesfield Grammar School, we have already met. For some reason they chose to keep the marriage secret until the scandal of Ellen's abduction became public knowledge.

During those intervening three years father and son dreamed of gaining seats in Parliament. The elder Wakefield was a friend of John Stuart Mill, the philosopher and radical, and had introduced Mill to Francis Place, the reformer who was working for the repeal of the Combination Laws. Wakefield senior had sat on two Parliamentary commissions and had written "An account of Ireland Statistical and Political". The younger Wakefield wished to enter the parliamentary fray in order to help Canning with his work towards Catholic Emancipation and the repeal of the Corn Laws. But to become a Member of Parliament was an expensive undertaking. The support of local worthies had to be ensured and at the election itself, the electorate expected a great deal of free liquid refreshment in return for their votes.

Wakefield junior could not afford his current lifestyle, his wife's money had passed to her children. Money would have to be secured from somewhere if he was to fund an election campaign and the obvious source was remarriage. But to whom? A wealthy widow? An heiress? But how would a family with the requisite money react to an impecunious young widower with two small children? He was not much of a catch! However he had already succeeded with one wealthy heiress by presenting her family with a fait accompli. Why not use the same ploy again?

That was where his new stepmother came in. Frances knew of a "suitable" young lady. Macclesfield, her home town, was just a few miles from Shrigley whose new owner had gained great wealth through trade. Might such a gentleman, making his way into high society, fear a scandal and so be reconciled to another of Wakefield's achievements?

The plot took just two weeks to hatch and it was believed by many commentators at the time that Frances Wakefield was its principal promoter. She certainly had the local knowledge and took part in the advance planning, though afterwards it seems she distanced herself from her two stepsons. Maybe she was more realistic and began to fear the consequences of their actions upon the future prospects of both her and her husband.

So it was that Frances took the boat from France and returned to Macclesfield and her father's house in December 1825. Maybe Dr Davies thought his dutiful daughter was home to spend the Christmas season with him. In fact Frances set about finding out as much as she could about the intended victim's family and, unwittingly, everyone she approached was willing to talk - for are not we all guilty of expressing an interest in newcomers to the district? What possible harm could there be in a little gossip? But what she discovered about William Turner and his circumstances was enough to convince Edward Gibbon Wakefield that Ellen should be his next victim.

Frances goes to Work

When Frances Wakefield returned to Macclesfield in December 1825 the silk industry was in depression and there were many signs of hardship to be seen. "The Macclesfield Courier" reported that the number of looms in the town had virtually halved from 5325 to 2279.[1] Whole columns were taken up with notices of bankruptcies. Even more alarm was caused when it was rumoured that the Bank of England itself had failed and local banks were in trouble. Robert Turner and Thomas Grimsditch amongst others promised publicly to honour notes issued by the two local banks.[2] Charitable funds were set up for the relief of depressed operatives (William Turner's name figures in the list of donors of money) and the ladies of the town promised to do their bit by wearing more silk.

Conditions in the town contrasted strongly with those Frances found about five miles away in the tiny Cheshire hamlet of Pott Shrigley. At his country seat, Shrigley Park, William Turner was a man demonstrating his success by building himself a country mansion from the proceeds of a thriving business.

He came from Blackburn in Lancashire where his family was already well known. His great grandfather, a farmer, set himself up as a chapman or dealer at Martholme, a nearby village. The business prospered and two of his grandsons, William and Robert, were each able to make their living out of one part of it. William stayed at Martholme and looked after the family's long established farm whilst Robert expanded the dealing side by moving to Mill Hill in Blackburn and setting up a calico printing firm on the banks of the River Darwen.

But the two brothers and their growing families were still very much a unit when it came to their businesses and family relationships. Together six of the family established a fulling mill at Helmshore in the

---

[1] "Macclesfield Courier" 11/2/1826
[2] Ibid 18/2/1826

Turner of

Blackburn & Helmshore

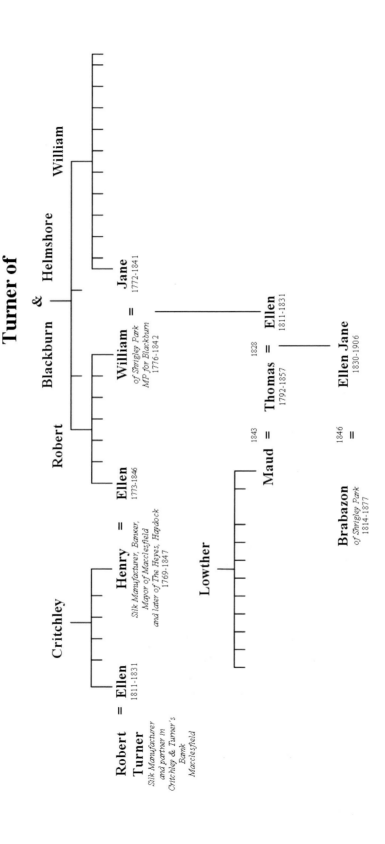

William

Robert

Critchley

William
of Shrigley Park
MP for Blackburn
1776-1842

Jane
1772-1841

Henry =
Silk Manufacturer, Banker,
Mayor of Macclesfield
and later of The Heyes, Haydock
1769-1847

Ellen
1773-1846

Robert = **Ellen**
Turner   1811-1831
Silk Manufacturer
and partner in
Critchley & Turner's
Bank
Macclesfield

Lowther

1828
Thomas = **Ellen**
1792-1857   1811-1831

1843
Maud =

Ellen Jane
1830-1906

1846
Brabazon =
of Shrigley Park
1814-1877

Rossendale area, now a working museum. Eventually William's side of the family took over sole control of this enterprise.

The two sides of the family were re-united when Robert's son, William, married his Uncle William's daughter, Jane. Whether this was a love match or business expediency we shall probably never know. Their daughter, Ellen, was to become the object of Wakefield's plot to gain a wealthy wife.

As the business in Blackburn thrived, so William's wealth and his standing in the locality grew. He and his surviving brothers, Robert, Thomas and John were regarded as local worthies, for upon them depended the livelihoods of much of the town's workforce. In times of depression it was to them that the town looked for charitable relief. In times of celebration it was to their premises that the crowds went to express their joy.

By the end of the Napoleonic Wars William had a fortune but one essential constituent of a successful business man eluded him. He had no son to inherit all his enterprises. In 1811 when his daughter Ellen was born, William was thirty five and Jane was thirty nine. Another daughter followed but died when she was four. William may have been in his prime but Jane was fast reaching the end of her child-bearing capabilities. A healthy son seemed improbable, so the only solution was to look for a suitable son-in-law. But what constituted "suitable"? For many a newly rich businessman the answer would be to look to a superior social class. Was that why the Turners bought Shrigley Park in 1818? Were they trying to climb the social ladder by buying a country estate at a good distance from their business enterprises so they could play the part of county gentry?

They were already familiar with Macclesfield because William's sister Ellen and her husband Henry Critchley lived there, at New Church Ground now part of Roe Street.[3] Critchley had been the town's mayor in 1807.[4] He and Robert Turner, his sister Elizabeth's husband, owned a bank which traded from 1802 until it failed in 1816.[5] In the 1850s he and another business partner ran a silk business which exhibited its wares at the Great Exhibition.[6]

[3] "Pigot's Directory" 1830

[4] J.P.Earwaker. "East Cheshire" 1880

[5] Stella Davies "History of Macclesfield"

[6] Ibid.

The Old Shrigley Hall

Carol Christian

Shrigley Hall 1850

"Mansions of England & Wales" Cheshire Vol 11 Twycross. 1850. Stovin & Bartlett

Frances would have known of much of the Turners' background before she really started investigating them for the purposes of the plot by the Wakefields. Her father from 1804 to 1811 was Vicar of Pott Shrigley. So Dr Davies must have known all about William Turner's newly acquired country seat. But she needed to know much more detail about the Turners and their movements. She had one more card up her sleeve. As the daughter of a well known local man she mixed with other notable families in the town. The wives and daughters of the gentry took tea with each other, organised charitable committees and, inevitably, exchanged gossip. It was a fairly close-knit community, they all knew each other. So her next move was to turn to her friends and to one unsuspecting friend in particular.

Ann Brocklehurst lived with her husband at Tytherington, just outside Macclesfield. She was a friend of Ellen's mother, Jane Turner, and used to take tea with her. It was an opportunity not to be missed. Frances would have had no difficulty in persuading Ann to take her to meet Mrs Turner. What could be more natural than to introduce two mutual friends? Mrs Turner was a semi-invalid so Frances' tales of her prolonged stay in France would surely please a lady whose own opportunities for excursions were limited. And, of course, Frances would be interested to encounter a potential new friend. There would certainly be no lack of conversation at such a meeting. So Ann Brocklehurst took Frances to tea at Shrigley with Jane Turner and unwittingly played her part in the plot.

That visit, late in February 1826, confirmed what Frances already knew - that the Turners were exceedingly wealthy. The old house had been partially demolished and the new mansion, which was virtually complete, had been added to the remaining portion. Its position was certainly splendid. From its huge central portico the eye was drawn through wooded hills down to the green of the Cheshire plain and on still further to the dim outline of the hills of Wales. The rooms took full advantage of this beautiful view whilst the internal opulent decor almost rivalled that of neighbouring Lyme Hall and left the visitor in no doubt of the owner's pretensions to grandeur. This was indeed quite a change from the old Hall and must have set quite a few local tongues wagging about the intentions of the new squire of Shrigley.

Then of course there was the news that William Turner had been appointed High Sheriff. Only an exceedingly wealthy man could afford the massive expense that this post entailed. The appointment had been announced in the "Macclesfield Courier" of February 4th. What a chance for the locals to view the new mansion for the Turners would be expected to give a sumptuous public breakfast before Mr Turner was escorted in procession to Chester to take up his duties.

Frances asked after Miss Turner and discovered that for the last five years she had been at a boarding school for young ladies in Toxteth, run by the Misses Daulby. On the 12th of the month Ellen had celebrated her fifteenth birthday at home and then, a few days later, her father had taken her back to school. Frances expressed some interest in Ellen and said she would like to meet her, but that would not have been an unusual sentiment, rather it would have appeared a form of politeness, given the circumstances of that afternoon.

So Frances had gained access to Shrigley and an introduction to Mrs Turner which meant subsequent visits would arouse no great surprise. This was important, for further visits were certainly planned!

Plans are Laid

At the very end of February Edward Gibbon Wakefield and his younger brother William arrived to stay with Dr Davies and Frances at their home in King Edward Street. They spent the next five days getting to know the area and devising their plot. No doubt Frances told them all she had discovered about the Turners and their daughter. She also took them riding on land belonging to the Leghs of Adlington, Shrigley itself and also into Thomas Legh's Lyme Park, the estate which bordered Shrigley. As present day visitors would ask for opening times at a tourist information centre, so the three riders made sure of their details. They actually rode to Thomas Grimsditch's office in the town to ask him where they could ride and to make arrangements for them to view Adlington Hall. The obliging Grimsditch contacted the Housekeeper at Adlington and the visit was arranged, although their timings went astray and the nearest they got to entry was ringing the doorbell!

On Saturday, March 4th, whether by accident or design is not known, Grimsditch met Frances in the street. This time he really fell into a trap. Frances managed to start him talking about the Turners and his indiscretion set the seal on Ellen's fate. All he said was that lately Mr Turner had had to spent time away from home in Blackburn, settling the affairs of his brother who had recently died, and that he and Mr Turner were just about to go to London on business for a few days. This was just the opportunity for which the plotters were waiting. They sprang into action.

Money was the first priority. On Sunday Frances sent a note to Brocklehurst's Bank just along the street and they sent Robert Bagshaw to the house to service her request. He gave her £150 made up of one note for £50, one bank post-bill for £60 and eight £5 Bank of England notes. Very carefully he recorded all their numbers and Frances signed for their receipt. Bagshaw remembered that Wakefield had jokingly likened Frances' action to that of signing her will.

The same evening Edward and William Wakefield, accompanied by their French servant, Thevenot, made as if to leave Macclesfield for London via Congleton. But in fact their destination was Manchester. At six o'clock on Monday morning Edward Gibbon Wakefield, calling himself Captain Wilson, arrived in Manchester on the Wilmslow post chaise. He booked into the Albion Hotel which stood at the corner of Oldham Street and Piccadilly. (The site now houses an amusement arcade). Four hours later he bought a dark green coach, a barouche,

Reproduced by kind permission of Lord Newton & Greater Manchester County Record Office

from William Carr, a coachmaker of Lower King Street. It was in need of repair, so Capt. Wilson paid £2 deposit and left. When he returned in mid-afternoon the work was unfinished so he gave orders for it to be delivered to the Albion Hotel by the early evening. At seven o'clock the coach arrived and was paid for with a £60 bank post-bill. Carr gave £20 change and returned the deposit to Captain Wilson.

Some time in the evening Thevenot was sent back to Macclesfield, presumably with a message for Frances. He went via Bullock Smithy, now called Hazel Grove, and when he arrived in Macclesfield asked the way to Park House, the home of Mr Ryle, a banker. However he was seen to go in another direction towards the home of Dr Davies. Before very long he was back at the chaise wanting to return to Manchester immediately. However he had to sit in the chaise and wait until the horses had eaten their corn and were fit enough to undertake the return journey.

Meanwhile Grimsditch and Mr Turner were on their way to London. At Shrigley the delicate Mrs Turner, supported by her sister-in-law, Mrs Critchley, was left in charge of the preparations for the public breakfast and the on-going building work. At Toxteth, no doubt, it had just been another day with every expectation that Ellen's schooling would continue as normal. It was only a few hours before all their lives became living nightmares.

At two o'clock in the morning on Tuesday, March 7th the barouche carrying Edward, William and Thevenot left the Albion Hotel and took the road to Liverpool. Capt Wilson had hired the horses and two post boys from the Albion to drive them. One of these men, Joshua Richards, had driven Thevenot to Macclesfield and back in the previous evening, now his task was to drive to Irlam. Throughout the long journey ahead the horses seem to have been watered every six miles and changed every twelve with, of course, new post boys being paid by Capt. Wilson to drive them. Once at Irlam the post boys would have awaited travellers in the opposite direction to drive back to their base.

From Irlam the party went on to Warrington and the Nag's Head where they left William. Jane Hughes, the landlady recalled the coach arriving at about four in the morning and that she gave William breakfast. Thevenot and his master were driven to Prescott and the Legs of Man. A new postboy, James Brown, drove on from there into the outlying area of Liverpool. They approached the city along West Derby Road and arrived at the Blue Bell where they were told they had come too far and were redirected. They turned back and went along Islington where Edward Gibbon Wakefield alighted from the coach leaving Thevenot alone to carry out the abduction.

As we have seen, it was the letter purporting to be from a Dr Ainsworth which had deceived the Daulbys into letting Ellen go with Thevenot. The author of the letter can only be guessed at now because it was never discussed at the trial. But neither was it stated why Thevenot had made the journey to Macclesfield the previous evening. Was it perhaps to pick up a suitable letter composed and written by Frances? We will never know.

So Ellen was handed into the carriage with Thevenot taking up his position on the dickey-box at the front. The kidnapping had succeeded and Ellen now began a long, long journey of over 600 miles over bumpy, pot-holed roads never quite knowing what was going to happen next. There were five days of continual travel during which time she only had three nights' sleep. Had this been a love match the seizure would have been romantic. But Ellen had never met her abductor, she must have been terrified when she realised she was not on her way back to Shrigley.

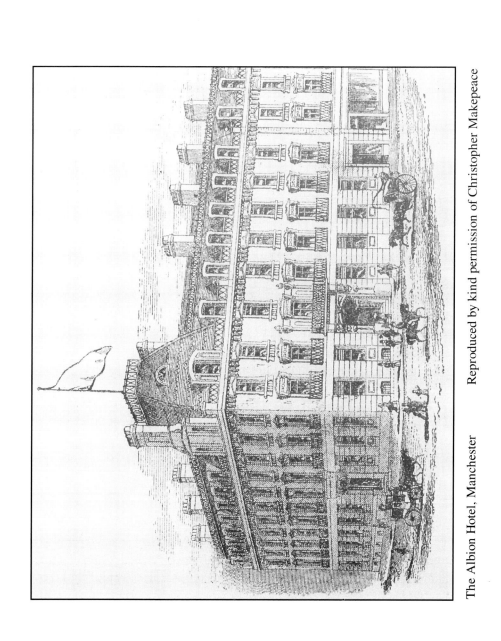

The Albion Hotel, Manchester

Reproduced by kind permission of Christopher Makepeace

The Journey

From Liverpool Ellen was taken via Warrington to Manchester where the barouche arrived at the Albion Hotel about mid-day. This was familiar territory for her because the Turners of Helmshore had their office just down the road. Ellen's uncle, Edward Turner, lived at Woodlands on the outskirts of the city and looked after this office. Her father's brother, Robert to whom she was the heir, also lived just along Oldham Street. She thought she was still on her way back to her home, so as yet she had no cause to feel alarmed.

Robert Wilson, the landlord, opened the carriage door and showed her up to the first floor. The room had two windows, one looked out across what is now Piccadilly Gardens towards the old Infirmary building, the other looked out onto the bustle of Oldham Street. A few yards away was the servants' room but Thevenot had given instructions that, if Ellen rang the bell, he would answer it. The servants from the hotel were not to attend her without his permission.

Ellen's physical needs were met throughout the journey. At each staging post serving women would escort the ladies from their carriages into a room in the inn where behind screens the necessary facilities would be found. If the ladies did not travel with their own maids then it was the serving maids' task to see that their visitors had all they needed. Food too was readily available at all hours. At the Albion the Housekeeper was ordered to bring Ellen a tart and custard.

Meanwhile the Wakefields made their way back to Manchester having kept in touch via notes (some of them in French) left at the Nag's Head in Warrington. They met up again at the Albion. About an hour after Ellen's arrival at the hotel, John Wilson, a waiter, showed Captain Wilson into the room and introduced him to his victim. Wilson said that Ellen advanced to meet the supposed Captain and they shook hands without Ellen showing any fear. But she had no reason to be afraid, as far as she knew she was on her way home to help her mother. Captain

Wilson explained the delay by saying that the story of Ellen's mother was not true but that the real person in trouble was Ellen's father due to the failure of the bank with which his business dealt. He said that Mr Turner had instructed him to take her to Blackburn where she and her father could safely meet.

To Ellen this would have been a feasible story. Bank failures were not exactly uncommon, her uncle's had ceased trading, and the consequences were disastrous. Secrecy was important in order to save ailing businesses before panic set in. She had also experienced the effects on one of her school friends, a Miss Greenwood who had recently been removed from school because of the same thing happening to her father. Mr Turner had even jokingly referred to the possibility on returning her to Toxteth a few weeks ago, when he had had difficulty in finding his money to pay her fees. Ellen's uncle had just died in Blackburn, her other uncle, Robert had his business there, so it was a good story with which to take in the young girl.

Madeira was called for and brought up to the room by another waiter, John Houlgrave. Then Capt. Wilson, William Wakefield, Thevenot and Ellen went down to the carriage in Oldham Street. Capt. Wilson made sure that the blinds were not in use so there was nothing secretive or suspicious to attract attention. But Ellen did not know that the post boys had been ordered to drive through Oldham to Delph, not towards Blackburn. William Wakefield and Thevenot took their places on the box, Ellen and Capt. Wilson sat inside the carriage and the post boys stirred the four horses into action.

So the journey northwards began. The constant movement and jolting was to continue right through the night and on until the following afternoon without a pause for either rest or sleep. From the evidence given at the trial their route is fairly easy to trace. Nothing is known of where the horses were changed at Oldham, but at Delph they stopped at the Blue Bell Inn which still serves travellers using the main road a little to the south of the village. There, as with most of the other stops, the postboys would have driven through the arched entrance into the inn yard and new horses would have been hired from the stables and put into the shafts for the next stage. If refreshment was needed the passengers would go into the inn, sometimes drink or food was brought out for them to consume in the carriage.

Richard Steele and Fairman were the postboys who drove the next stage to Huddersfield with a watering stop at Marsden. By now the terrain was becoming hilly. When going uphill became too difficult for the horses, the gentlemen passengers would be expected to dismount and walk. The George at Huddersfield was reached by about 7.30 in the evening. The hotel was in the market place but it was later rebuilt in St Peter's Street and is now used as offices.

Here a problem arose. The landlord, Mr Wigney, remembered that the gentlemen wished to change horses and depart immediately, but the servant had said that it was impossible because a broken spring on the coach needed mending before they went any further. The repair took about three quarters of an hour, so the party were shown into a room. Mary Brock, the chambermaid, took the young lady into the sitting room to attend to her needs after which Charles Croft, a waiter, had taken in tea and bread and butter to them all. He had seen the gentleman pour the hot water to make the tea. When they went the young lady had come down on the gentleman's arm and the chambermaid had opened the carriage door for them. William Langstaff and his companion then took the reins for the next stage of the journey to Halifax.

By this time Ellen must have realised she was not being taken to Blackburn. We only have her abductor's version of how she was persuaded to continue the journey. Wakefield said that he told her that her father was being forced to move northwards to escape his creditors and that they were to meet him eventually.

Gradually he also introduced another element, saying he had a wealthy uncle who was a banker and this uncle would be willing to rescue Ellen's father from his financial predicament if Ellen would marry Wakefield. To the twenty first century reader of the story this may seem a rather far-fetched tale but Ellen would have known the awful consequences of financial ruin. Her friend, Miss Greenwood, had been removed from school after her father's business collapsed. Ellen's Uncle Henry had been saved from financial ruin by being able to pay his creditors a percentage of what he owed them. Macclesfield was full of failed businesses. Then there was her father's standing in Cheshire. If he was disgraced it would put an end to his position of High Sheriff and also to all his plans for her. She must have known she was being groomed for marriage to someone of her father's choice and that she was expected to provide a male heir for both her father's and uncle's businesses. Surely a marriage which saved her father's reputation and business would be just what he wanted. Though we may find her presumed willingness strange, to the young heiress, deprived of sleep as she was, maybe it was a very plausible option.

At Halifax the carriage stopped at the White Lion on Silver Street. The street still exists but its early nineteenth century buildings have been replaced. The only trace of the White Lion is on an 1868 drawing.[1]

Thomas Issot, who was the waiter there, described their arrival at nine o'clock. Thevenot left for London taking some luggage and just one of the other gentlemen had gone into the Inn. By this time, of course, it was pitch dark but, by the light of the gas lights, Issot had recognised Ellen as a young lady who had dined there with her father about eight weeks previously.

One wonders at his expertise in remembering faces since thousands must have visited the inn which was on a very busy route. But then much of the evidence was presented in a very glib fashion as we will see later.

By nine thirty a new post boy, Henry Mason, was watering the horses at Keighley. The next stop to be recalled by any of the witnesses was at the Devonshire Arms in Skipton. Ann Bradley, who kept the hotel, said the party arrived at ten o'clock. They stayed in the carriage whilst new horses were ordered for Settle. Mrs Bradley told the maidservant to take them out gingerbread and two glasses of water. The maid had put the cake onto Ellen's lap. Now they were well on their way to the border and Mrs Bradley had her suspicions of an elopement. She had said she would be glad to welcome them to her inn on their return.

The Golden Lion at Settle, kept by Mr Hartley, was reached about one thirty in the morning. Here the horses and post boys were changed again.

The party drove on to the Rose and Crown in Kirby Lonsdale. This inn was new, for in 1820 the previous building had been destroyed

---

[1]Silver Street from Hall End. 1868. J. R. Smith. Illustration in Halifax Library.

in a fire.[2] It stands in the market place of this bustling little town. Sarah Coltman, a maid, must have been half asleep when she stumbled over the doorstep sometime between three and four in the morning on her way to the carriage. Her clumsy action had amused the party, but she also remembered the young lady commenting on how favourable the weather was for it was warm for that time of year though misty.

Edward Garratt drove from there to Kendal arriving about five thirty at the King's Arms. This inn has long since disappeared but was at the top of Finkle Street.[3] Hannah Simpson, a chambermaid, took the party breakfast in the sitting room. The lady had retired on her own to a bedroom for about twenty minutes. When Garratt went to their room to be paid he saw the lady and gentleman walking backwards and forwards about the room side by side. Stretching one's legs must have been essential after fifteen hours of continuous coach travel. And there was more to come!

Now came the bleakest part of the journey. Robert Dover drove from Kendal to Shap, high up in the desolate fells, a little village which had sheltered travellers for centuries until bypassed by the building of the M6. The actual inn where the horses were changed is not known but James Anderson was hired there to drive them on to Penrith and was paid six shillings for his work on their arrival.

Here the horses were changed at the Crown, an inn which no longer exists.[4] There the waiter, James Hamilton, remembered them only stopping for ten minutes, they did not even have any refreshment. By ten thirty in the morning Edward Baxter was driving them towards Carlisle which they reached around midday.

The coach stopped for a quarter of an hour at the Bush, kept by Mrs Sarah Holmes. The inn was used for important occasions such as the dinner for the High Sheriff the previous year when Mr Holmes was reported to have "procured a very lively Turtle for the occasion,

---

[2] Queen Adelaide stayed there in 1840 and it was renamed the Royal in her honour.

[3] Oil-painting by Stirzaker, 1823, showing King's Arms reproduced in "Kirbie-Kendal" J. F. Curwen. Kendal Library

[4] Photographs of it have been published in "Penrith in Times Past" Lawrence Marlow. 1987

weighing 80 pounds." [5] Redevelopment of the town centre has obliterated any trace of the Bush.

The gentlemen left the coach but when the head waiter, Thomas Atkinson, went to help the lady alight one of the gentlemen said she was not leaving the carriage. Atkinson asked if horses were required for Gretna and was told they were.

It was in Carlisle that Wakefield had told Ellen that she would meet her father. So he then had to explain Turner's absence to Ellen. Fortunately for Wakefield there was a boisterous crowd outside the inn. A crowd was not unusual for a great many eloping couples called here before they made the crossing into Scotland. Sometimes pursuing relatives appeared and the crowd witnessed an exciting chase or a battle for possession, quite a spectator sport for the local townsfolk. Wakefield told Ellen that her father and Grimsditch were indeed in the inn but that the crowd was composed of creditors and that her father had begged for Ellen to marry Wakefield as quickly as possible and so save the situation. What more could a loving, concerned daughter do other than to obey her father? So Ellen became the submissive dupe.

William Graham was the postboy on the last stage of their journey across the border to Gretna. He was quite used to driving eloping couples and knew where to take them. He drove through the village to Gretna Hall where one of the gentlemen climbed down and asked if this was where the parson was. Graham told him that the marriage would be performed in the Hall but it usually took about half an hour for the parson to be summoned. The landlord of Gretna Hall, John Linton came out and took the group inside. A servant showed the men into one small room and the lady into another whilst a fire was lit in the drawing room. The lady was then left alone whilst the men went out, presumably to await the arrival of the parson. Everything was now ready for a commonplace happening in Gretna, but it was far from mundane for the fifteen year old heiress from Pott Shrigley.

---

[5] "Round Carlisle Cross. Famous Carlisle Hostelries" Local History Unit files, Carlisle Library.

Marriage

Lord Hardwicke's Act of 1754 made the law in England pertaining to marriages much stricter than it had been. Couples had to marry in church and had to have the consent of their parents if they were under twenty one. All marriages had to be recorded in the register and signed by both parties. However in Scotland, once any couple had declared themselves husband and wife before witnesses, the marriage was deemed to be legal. This led to a great number of elopements by couples whose parents were opposed to their marriage. The establishment in 1777 of a turnpike road over the river Sark, the border between the two countries, meant that the tiny communities of Springfield and Gretna were the first villages eloping couples reached in their flight north.

But the turnpike road was also used by the coaches taking travellers between London and Scotland. Their appearance necessitated coaching houses where the travellers could find food and refreshment and where the horses could be changed. Thus it was in 1793 that Gretna Hall was converted into an inn. It must have been one of the most pleasant settings for an inn along the whole route. Rather than being alongside the road, the Hall is approached along a driveway lined with trees and shrubs and has a pleasant rural outlook towards the Solway Firth.

In 1825 John Linton, who had been valet to Sir James Graham and knew how the gentry expected to be treated, took the lease of the inn which soon acquired a reputation for its hospitality. In the next thirty years there were 1,134 marriages recorded in the register kept at the Hall so eloping couples must have contributed quite a tidy sum to his takings. Some couples were obviously virtually penniless, some were decidedly affluent. Records show that Linton's fees varied from 10/6 to £20.

The buildings which still host marriage ceremonies have been considerably extended to cater for the enormous number of tourists who flock to see Gretna Green. The original Hall where Ellen and Wakefield were married is still discernible and it is easy to locate the rooms used by the pair that day.

Evidence given at the trial gives us a vague picture of the few hours the couple spent at Gretna Hall. John Linton's sister, Frances, was sent upstairs to light a fire in the sitting room and Ellen was installed there. The Wakefields awaited the parson's arrival downstairs and William Graham would have fed and watered the horses in the stables just across the yard before being called to the hall to take his usual part in the proceedings.

It took about half an hour for David Laing, the "parson" to arrive from his home in Springfield. He was seventy one and had lived an interesting life before finding this very lucrative occupation. He had been a pedlar in Lancashire from where he had been press ganged onto a navy ship which had been captured by John Paul Jones. He had escaped when Jones was on a smuggling expedition sailing along the Solway coast close to Springfield, Laing's birthplace. In 1792 he started marrying eloping couples and proudly boasted that none of the marriages which he had performed had been found invalid in the courts. After Laing's death his son Simon and then his grandson William continued the trade.

Laing asked the couple their names and addresses and they duly swore in front of him, that they took each other as husband and wife with John Linton and William Graham, as witnesses. A certificate and

---

- 1826 -

Gretna Hall Marriage Register.-

Edward Gibbon Wakefield from the parish of St James's London, County of Middlesex,

To Ellen Turner from the parish of Pott Shrigley and the County of Chester.

Jno Linton   *David Laing,*
Wm Graham } *Witnesses,*

March 8th,

the register entry were made out.[1] As far as Edward Gibbon Wakefield was concerned Ellen was now his lawful wife and her fortune was his to control. Ellen thought that by agreeing to marry Wakefield she had saved her father from financial and social ruin. She must have been both satisfied and relieved to have done what she regarded as the duty of a loving daughter. She had been travelling since early the previous morning, could she now relax?

According to Laing a meal was ordered and his advice was sought on which wines were available. This sounds highly improbable given the couple's background but, out of the three or four he knew Linton kept, he said that "shumpine" was the best. He left the new Mr and Mrs Wakefield, presumably with William, to enjoy their wedding breakfast. At the end of their meal he rejoined them and they finished off the wine. He told Ellen that it was the custom to give him a present for his trouble and she gave him twenty shillings as a note and told him to buy a pair of gloves.

After payments had been made by Wakefield to Laing and Linton, the newly married Wakefields were back on the road again but this time heading south. At Carlisle they again stopped at the Bush Inn at about six o'clock. Here their coach was declared unfit to carry them any further and was sent to a coachmakers. They took tea and Wakefield wrote to his father's clerk with instructions to insert the wedding announcement in "The Times" and also to his father to tell him he was married, but gave no details of his bride. Was this an oversight or did his father know beforehand what his son's plans were? After two hours they left for Penrith in a post chaise.

James Hamilton remembered them arriving at Penrith about eleven o'clock. Three separate rooms were ordered for the night and arrangements were made for them to travel on the next day by the mail coach. He also recalled Wakefield changing a £50 note. The following morning Ellen came down first and read until the two gentlemen joined her for breakfast. They spent the next night in Leeds and parted from William who was despatched to Shrigley to tell Ellen's father of the wedding. Some reports say that he could find no one at home and left a message which was never delivered, others say he visited Frances in Macclesfield before going on to London.

---

[1] A register was sold by auction at Christie's in July 2002. British Trust Hotels, the group which owns Gretna Hall, paid £7,637 for it and intend to put it on display. The illustration is taken from it and reproduced with permission.

Meanwhile Ellen and her new husband reached Blake's Hotel[2] in Hanover Square, London late on Saturday night. There they met a man called Mills who advised Wakefield in no uncertain terms to make his way to France with all speed or face arrest. Virtually as soon as they arrived they were departing for the ferry across the Channel where the new husband and his younger brother would find comparative safety.

Thus the story of the abduction is as complete as we can make it, considering the available evidence. Ellen was rescued and the story was public knowledge. But there is an additional twist to our tale and it was to prove significant for later events.

Edward Gibbon was not the only Wakefield with marriage in mind. William too had found a bride, the daughter of Sir John Sydney of Penshurst.[3] They had met a year earlier and negotiations with Sir John over financial arrangements had started when Ellen's abduction, aided and abetted by William, was being planned and executed. Just eighteen days after the wedding at Gretna, William was married in Paris before the marriage settlement had been agreed. So William was in Paris and his father-in-law in England where the press were beginning to revel in every detail, true or imagined, of the recent abduction. Not the best of starts to any marriage.

We must now turn to the press to follow events for the next twelve months.

---

[2] Some reports say it was the Brunswick Hotel. Did Blake own it?

[3] Her forename remains as yet a mystery, even her obituary omits it.

The Press Starts Its Coverage

If one compares the papers of the time, it very soon becomes apparent
that they simply used reports in other papers to fill their own. Thus the
initial marriage announcement appeared in "The Times", a national
paper based in London. That paper was then carried through England
along the various coaching routes, reaching all parts surprisingly
quickly. A Macclesfield coaching house boasted that it had the London
papers by ten a.m. The story was taken up by the press in Blackburn,
Manchester, Stockport and Macclesfield where the Turners were
known. But it was printed by papers across the country when it
promised interesting scandal.

The announcement was made on Saturday, March 11th. Four
days later the "Blackburn Mail" repeated it with a local slant (and a
slight inaccuracy),

> *"On the 6th inst Edward Gibbon Wakefield Esq to Ellen only*
> *daughter of William Turner Esq formerly of Mill House near this*
> *town and now of Shrigley Park Cheshire and High Sheriff of that*
> *county"[1]*

A week later they quoted from the London "Courier's" report
stating that the marriage was the result of a cruel case of abduction and
that the original announcement had been submitted to a newspaper
agency office by Mr Wakefield, Surveyor of Pall Mall. The report
continued with a description of Ellen as a young lady of quick natural
talents and that

> *"no pains have been spared upon their cultivation. Her affection for*
> *her parents is unbounded, of which her conduct throughout this*
> *recent affair is a striking example."[2]*

In theory, when they found out that the supposed wedding had
been an abduction, the Macclesfield "Courier" should have had a distinct

---

[1] "Blackburn Mail" 15 / 3 / 1826
[2] Ibid   22 / 3 / 1826

advantage because Thomas Grimsditch, its proprietor, was privy to all the details of the true story. But he was the trusted friend and agent for the Turner family. He had already been duped into revealing details about Turner's movements to Miss Davies and now he was occupied helping Turner present the best case against the legality of the marriage. Discretion would have to be his watchword. So the "Courier" did not join in the press speculation and gossip. However it was to weigh into the fray to denigrate Wakefield as much as possible in order to get the public's sympathy firmly on William Turner's side. But it was difficult to resist a good story.

Just three days after Ellen had been found in Calais the following article appeared,

> *"The announcement in most of the London papers of the marriage of Miss Turner of Shrigley to Mr Edward Gibbon Wakefield has, from the extreme youth of the lady, excited a very considerable sensation in this part of the country. We have no disposition under the head of Elopement, to administer to the purient curiosity of the public, not at the expense of the feelings of the parties concerned, but as journalists we have a paramount duty to perform in thus stating what has come to our knowledge, suppressing, from motives of delicacy, a detail of the various rumours that are afloat, reflecting on the conduct of the gentleman who plays so conspicuous part in the transaction...........from every enquiry which the friends of Miss Turner have been able to make, there appears no proof of any previous aquaintainship (sic) between the parties........The affair has already assumed too serious an aspect to be passed over in silence; the friends of this young lady have taken measures for the purpose of insuring the fullest investigation, and doubtless the facts will ere long be made public, til when we shall abstain from all comment."*[3]

A masterpiece of understatement or of innuendo?

Six days later the Stockport "Advertiser" announced that the High Sheriff, who had previously said he would have to cancel the public breakfast, had changed his mind,

> *"The happy frustration of the late diabolical attempt upon the peace of his family, in the abduction of his daughter, has led to this change. He will leave Shrigley Park for Chester on Saturday 1ˢᵗ April at 12.00 with numerous friends."*[4]

---

[3] "Macclesfield Courier" 18 / 3 / 1826
[4] "Stockport Advertiser" 24 / 3 / 1826

The "Courier" gave more details adding that the departure would be preceded by the planned public breakfast. That was a trifle indiscreet in the circumstances. Here was a newly built mansion, itself an object of local curiosity, which was to throw open its doors. Might Miss Turner, the lately abducted heiress, be present?

But then came a breakthrough for the Turners and of course the ever hungry press. William Wakefield had to return to England to see his new father-in-law and was promptly arrested at Dover on Tuesday, 28th of March just two days after his marriage. He was taken into custody and brought through Macclesfield to Stockport where he was kept overnight on the Thursday at the house of Barrett, the Constable. The following morning at the Rams Head in Disley he appeared before three local magistrates, Thomas Legh of Lyme, S.P. Humphreys of Bramhall, and G.J. Newton of Taxal Lodge near Whaley Bridge.

The hearing report appeared a week later in the local papers.[5] Dr Davies and a solicitor gave character references and offered bail. Ellen was called to be questioned about the abduction and how she had been deceived into marrying by the story of her father's financial failure. Mr Grimsditch said he had never spoken or written to the Wakefields before the 15th of the month when he had written to E.G. Wakefield asking for the return of Ellen's clothes. (Had he forgotten meeting him in Macclesfield?) William Turner's evidence was intended to undermine the supposed legality of the marriage as well as to show Wakefield's offence. He told the magistrates that Ellen was only fifteen, that she was his only child and his heir apparent. The hearing then had to be adjourned to the following Monday until Miss Daulby could be summoned from Toxteth.

On their way to Disley the poor Miss Daulbys had an accident.
" the forewheel of the chaise came off between Manchester and Stockport and the chaise fell to the ground. In this dreadful situation the horses set off at full speed and after galloping for half a mile they were stopped by the carriage coming into contact with a post, when the ladies were released from their situation little worse for the accident."

Despite this ordeal Miss Elizabeth gave her evidence clearly. After describing how they had been duped into parting with Ellen, she said she and Miss Turner had never seen the Wakefields. Miss Turner

---

[5] "Macclesfield Courier"   8 / 4 / 1826

had only ever left the school to go to church or on walks with Miss Daulby or their friends.

Mr Harmer, representing Wakefield, only asked the magistrates what they intended to do. Mr Grimsditch's opinion was that Wakefield's crime was a capital offence and the prisoner must be committed for trial. Harmer's opinion was that the offence was a misdemeanour, in that the victim of the abduction was under sixteen, and that Mr Turner might well have a son in the future thus rendering Ellen only the heir apparent. Harmer quoted a statute of Philip and Mary to support his argument, Grimsditch countered with Edward 1 and said the magistrates had to decide whether or not to grant bail. They did not but committed William to gaol in Lancaster from where Harmer hoped a judge would bail him after the granting of a writ of habeas corpus.

William was indeed bailed a few days later. The battle lines had been drawn. The Turners were trying to retain both their fortune and Ellen's virtue intact so she could still make a good marriage with a suitable gentleman. The Wakefields were still intent on proving the validity of the marriage.

And once more there is a romantic version of the hearing which would have us believe that it was at the Rams Head that thirty four year old Thomas Legh of Lyme, the wealthy owner of vast estates, sitting as a magistrate, first saw the fifteen year old heiress as she gave her evidence. It could be true ....but let us continue with the facts before we consider how events came to pass.

The Breakfast

The ceremonial start of Turner's year as High Sheriff was on the
Saturday after the first hearing. All the speculation and reports in the
papers brought more people to Shrigley Hall than had been expected so
it proved somewhat hectic. Though it was called a public breakfast the
Turners were quite surprised when people arrived without invitations.
But compared to the torment of the last weeks this must have faded into
insignificance and the show went on - for show it most certainly was.

   The fullest account of the ceremonial is to be found in the
"Stockport Advertiser". The reporter praised Mr Turner for continuing
the traditional pomp at his own expense and dismissed the more recent
practice of using professional javelin men.[1] He went into raptures about
the food and wines freely consumed by two hundred gentlemen
downstairs, whilst Mrs Turner entertained their ladies upstairs with an
equal display of hospitality and elegance. Mr Lynn from the Waterloo
Inn in Liverpool, the gentleman who had been the caterer at the recent
Preston Guild, obviously did the Turners proud.

> *"The sideboard groaned beneath the weight of an enormous baron of
> beef, decorated in a style which excited the admiration of all guests.
> Immediately above it was placed the family crest (moulded in
> butter)..........In various parts of the table .... bannerets were
> displayed, interspersed with immense bouquets of French artificial
> flowers, which to every sense presented the appearance of reality.
> The confectionery both in detail and execution was equally graceful
> to the eye and the palate, the ices and jellies were in the greatest
> variety and of the most exquisite quality........Of the wines it is
> impossible to speak in adequate terms.Burgundy, Champagne, Hock,
> Claret, Madeira, Port, Sherry and Bucellas vied with each other in*

---

[1] Javelin men were pike or spear-carrying ceremonial escorts to judges on assize and
to High Sheriffs.

Shrigley Hall Interior 1850   "Mansions of England & Wales" Cheshire Vol 11 Twycross. 1850. Stovin & Bartlett

excellence, and the guests were not backward in acknowledging the merits of each...........[2]"

During the final stages of the banquet Thomas Legh proposed the first toast to the High Sheriff. That was followed by one to Mr Legh and the House of Lyme and then Mrs Turner's health was proposed.

By noon the breakfast was over and the procession was formed. Thomas Legh on horseback led one hundred of his tenants. Then came the Sheriff's Steward leading two trumpeters on cream chargers, their instruments bearing banners decorated with the Turner arms. Twenty two of Turner's tenants followed them acting as his javelin men in new suits, carrying halberts engraved with the Turner arms. Eight mounted sheriff's officers rode behind in new scarlet coats, buff waistcoats, white breeches and jockey boots. Mr Grimsditch, the under sheriff preceded William Turner who was followed by his valet, all on horseback. Then came the High Sheriff's new carriage drawn by four brown horses with the postillions in splendid new liveries. Two footmen rode behind it followed by thirty two carriages containing Mr Turner's friends. The last section of the procession consisted of one hundred and forty mounted gentlemen - a grand total of 238 men, mostly mounted, not counting all those in the carriages and the High Sheriff himself!

The cavalcade travelled through the tiny hamlet of Pott Shrigley, then Bollington and Macclesfield before it stopped at Broken Cross. Here Turner transferred to his carriage and most of the participants cheered him on his way to Chester before they made their way home. What a sight! What a day! What excitement for all the locals who turned out to watch.

And leading the toasts and heading the procession, with four times as many of his tenants compared with those mustered by the High Sheriff, was Thomas Legh of Lyme.

---

[2] "Stockport Advertiser" 7 / 4 / 1826

Temporary Respite

The Turners had one villain under the jurisdiction of the English legal system but their main target was still lurking safely in France. All they could do was to collect as much evidence against him and the validity of the marriage as was possible. Meanwhile the press carried on searching for every bit of gossip.

They now had Wakefield senior in their sights, after all, the announcement had come from his office. He was intending to become Reading's M.P. so the electors there were entitled to an explanation. He held a public meeting assuring the electorate that he knew nothing of the abduction before it had taken place, but he refused to condemn the actions of his son. The papers were not impressed. The raking up of scandal continued.

In mid April a marriage was announced,

"At the chapel of the British Embassy, in Paris, on 3rd August, 1823, Mr Edward Wakefield, of Pall Mall, London, to Frances, only daughter of the Rev. Dr. Davies, Head Master of the Free Grammar School, in Macclesfield."[1]

This announcement caused an extraordinary sensation in Macclesfield. Why had the wedding been kept secret for nearly three years? Rumours and speculation as to the couple's involvement in the abduction persisted until, eventually, Wakefield senior brought a case for libel against the "Reading Mercury" In the evidence a handbill was cited. It jokingly asserted that Wakefield would have the votes of all mistresses of schools for young girls and of parents wishing good marriages for their daughters. Wakefield lost his case and was dropped as candidate for Reading.

Then a letter from the abductor himself appeared in the London "Courier". He asserted that he would return from France as soon as his

---

[1] "Macclesfield Courier" 15 / 4 / 1826

business was completed. The Macclesfield "Courier" had its doubts and chose to make its point by lampooning the fugitive.

> *"Collection of Oddities. On Tuesday, Mr Gibbon Wakefield arrived at Lancaster in a balloon from Mile End, elegantly dressed in a salmon coloured pelisse, with a plume of ostrich feathers, and waited upon Prince Leopold in the anti-room at Northumberland House. He had his pockets full of pebbles and must have been under water several days. He was, however purchased by Mrs Coutts, for her villa at Highgate….."*[2]

No sooner had the Turners recovered their daughter than yet another blow struck the family. William's brother John, who had taken over the house at Mill Hill in Blackburn, fell ill. For three weeks he was in great pain and then died only eight months after their other brother Thomas. Ellen's role as heiress was even more important to all the remaining Turner family.

Ten days after the death was announced, a totally unexpected caller arrived at Taxal Lodge, the home of Mr Newton, which was situated in a small village just outside Whaley Bridge and only a few miles from Pott Shrigley. No-one was ready for him, but at last, Ellen's father and the man who claimed to be his lawful son-in-law met face to face.

---

[2] "Macclesfield Courier" 6 / 5 / 1826

Let Battle Commence

If Wakefield had stopped in France he would have stood a chance of remaining free from prosecution in England. But from abroad it would have been difficult for him to prove the marriage was legal and so to retain control over Ellen's inheritance. There had been an agreement that he would return and the Turner faction had prepared the requisite papers. However he had been expected three weeks before and it was assumed that he had changed his mind. So great a surprise was his return to England, it appears that the authorities did not notice and he made his own way northwards.

When he presented himself at Taxal Lodge on Tuesday, May 16th, Mr Newton could not immediately put him into custody without the relevant papers, so Wakefield became his guest overnight. The following morning at noon, William Turner arrived with his lawyer and swore an affidavit in front of Mr Newton who then placed Wakefield into the custody of the Constable of Stockport, Mr Barrett. Once that formality was over, a preliminary hearing started which heard evidence from Turner. Wakefield made no attempt to question his father-in-law. The solicitor asked for an adjournment to enable other witnesses to attend and this was granted. Wakefield was taken to Stockport in custody with *"every accommodation to be afforded to him by the police."*[1]

On the following Monday "John Bull" published a "Statement of facts regarding the marriage of Edward Gibbon Wakefield, Esq. with Miss Turner". Written in the first person, it is very long containing over seven thousand words. The introduction by the journal makes interesting reading. It apologises for inserting such a long document but judges that the statement is so curious that publishing it in full is justified. It continues

"We have often heard novel-writers…censured for the improbable

---

[1] "Macclesfield Courier" 20 / 5 /1826

conduct of their fictions, but we must beg to vindicate them from the charge, by submitting a tale of real life, which far surpasses every thing we ever met with in imaginary history."[2]

Wakefield described how, on a visit to Macclesfield, he heard much derogatory gossip about Mr Turner and his family, which seemed to arise out of envy of the newly arrived, wealthy gentleman. Miss Turner was said to be ugly, ignorant, awkward and vulgar. However he was told by the well-informed that she was pretty, clever, well-educated and most amiable. His first instinct had been to show his feelings against the envy of the general populace by joining in the High Sheriff's procession, but then, on an impulse, he had decided to marry Miss Turner as long as, when he met her he found he could cherish her, that she should want to marry him and that he could do so without using force or restraint.

He went on to describe how he had won Ellen's confidence during their journey,

"...we...talked incessantly...I behaved to her as I would to a beloved sister, whom I had joined, after separation...and whom my whole soul was bent on pleasing - with careful reserve...with intimacy without familiarity...with no more tenderness than any man of feeling would display to a helpless woman... that she was pleased I soon had ample proof."

At Halifax he said he told Thevenot, in French, to book family rooms at the Brunswick Hotel not realising that she spoke French.

He continued to work his charm,

"...before we reached Kendal, she treated me with all the affectionate confidence and gratifying intimacy that a cherished friend and admitted lover could have expected from her...She had passed one whole night with me and I could have urged that...she would do well to become my wife without delay....I dreaded to appear a brute in the eyes of this sweet girl...I had gone too far to recede...She entered, at once, and I may say eagerly, into what she thought a scheme for securing her father's fortune... There was no holding back, no hesitation."

He pointed out to her that she had not known him for long but she had said that she believed they would be happy and at that he had taken her in his arms and kissed her. From that moment he had treated her as his future wife and took care that the ceremony at Gretna was more formal than that which was generally performed there.

---

[2] "John Bull" 22 / 5 / 1826. Pp 165 & 166

Wakefield finished by saying he had been compelled to make the statement

> " *in order to remove from myself...and from my wife the mortifying imputations, which have been cast upon us both...It may be well to pursue me vindictively, but it is cruel to make her suffer for my sins. I will therefore trust that* (this statement) *may check, for the future, the well-meant though misguided zeal with which his* (Mr Turner's) *Agents have laboured, and are still striving to make his daughter a public laughing stock, and the object of everlasting curiosity and comment."*

The statement was followed by a letter signed by Wakefield and addressed to Turner. It was dated the 6th of May, ten days before he arrived at Taxal.

The day after the publication of the statement a full hearing took place at the Rams Head in Disley. Wakefield arrived in a chaise from Stockport about a quarter past eleven. The "Courier" described his *"happy flow of spirits which he describes to be his usual attendants".[3]* On arrival it appears he talked with Dr Davies whilst they walked on the green in front of the inn.

The "Courier" goes on to paint a picture of the scene at the hearing. The Turner family sat on one sofa, whilst Wakefield threw himself nearly at full length on a sofa at the other side of the fireplace *"ever and anon applying a silk handkerchief to his face."* Also in the room were the magistrates, Messrs Newton, Humphreys and Tatton of Wythenshawe, and thirty six members of the public.

Ellen's evidence, which she had given at the earlier hearing of William Wakefield's case, was read by the clerk, Mr Vaughan of Stockport then Elizabeth Daulby was called to repeat her testimony. Wakefield did not question her evidence. Next came Ellen herself, brought into the room by her father and dressed in deep mourning for her recently dead uncle.

Grimsditch tried to prove the marriage had taken place by deception by questioning Ellen. The fifteen year old replied,

> *"I went against my inclination, but it was from a desire to save my father. I consented to marry him (Wakefield) to save him; it was solely to serve my father, and to save him from ruin. He (Wakefield) said it was the only way, and I believed from his representations that it was so."*

---

[3] "Macclesfield Courier" 27 / 5 / 1826 which is the source of all the quotations from this hearing.

Next Grimsditch turned to the signing of the marriage certificate which Ellen had said she thought was a certificate which would save her father. Here Wakefield protested that this was not what he had given Ellen to understand. He was told he may put his observation in the form of a question, which he declined to do but one of the magistrates intervened to clear up the point and drew a more complete answer from Ellen.

> *"What sort of a Certificate was it? Was it a certificate that you consented to be married in consequence of the distress of your father?"*
> *"It was but I did not write it so. I understood it to be a certificate of my consent"*

Then Ellen was able to add to her evidence from the previous trial and again it was to emphasise Wakefield's deception She said that Wakefield had told her that a letter requesting her to marry was from Grimsditch and said she may not recognise the agent's usual writing because he was in a distressed state when he wrote it. Ellen had said she did not know Grimsditch's writing.

As Ellen was conducted out of the room by her father, Wakefield was the first to rise and he bowed his head slightly towards her.

Then it was Turner's turn to give evidence. He described receiving the first letter from Wakefield and then the others which were all delivered to Shrigley after Ellen had been recovered from France. The first had been written on the day after the couple's arrival at Calais. Wakefield wrote in the hope that he could heal the breech and to assure Turner that his daughter was in the best of health. He went on to say that, had the injury he had done been inflicted on him, he would have been furious but hoped that Turner would wait to find out all the facts before making any judgement. He acknowledged that he had taken on the most sacred of obligations to treat Ellen with devoted tenderness. Finally he said that Ellen was longing to see her father and

> *"watches every packet as if her life depended upon seeing you in it. She is a dear, affectionate, excellent creature, and well deserves from you as much affection as she feels towards you."*

The following day he wrote again saying that his friend would arrive the next day and all three would go to Paris. Then he had the cheek to accuse Turner of neglecting Ellen who could not understand why no letter had come from Shrigley to tell her how her mother was.

The day after Ellen was removed from him, he began his campaign to prove the marriage valid. He wrote to reprove Turner for his displeasure at the marriage and hoped that Ellen would be allowed to love him as she ought. He said he had taken *"the most religious care to treat her as his sister"*. He repeated these sentiments using, what the reporter called, pretty strong language,

> *"Perhaps it may be a further satisfaction to you to hear, that my intercourse with your daughter has been punctiliously delicate, and that I have treated her with the utmost reserve, not merely abstaining from the rights of a husband, but carefully guarding myself from taking any even the slightest liberty with her person; as well as from an allusion of any sort in conversation that would have been improper from a brother to a sister".*

He went on to recommend that Turner should not let his passion get the better of his considered judgement.

> *"You, Sir, have a question to decide ....It is that of your child's happiness or misery for the rest of her life."*

Unfortunately for Wakefield, Turner was already convinced he knew what would make his daughter happy - and it most certainly was not marriage to Wakefield.

Critchley was then called to give evidence and described in great detail the events which had taken place at the Hotel Quillac. From the boat he had seen Wakefield hurry Ellen from the quayside and had lost sight of them. Critchley made it clear that Wakefield had expected Ellen to favour her father's friends over him, which of course she did, calling Wakefield a brute. Whilst they waited for the police officer to come into the hotel room, Critchley had asked Wakefield what induced him to commit so flagrant and cruel an act, as to carry away so mere a child, whom he had never seen. The reply was straightforward,

> *"I have been a great deal with Dr Davies's family, where she had very frequently been the topic of conversation; she has been represented to me as a fine girl, with the largest fortune in the county, and I was therefore determined to possess myself of her, to accomplish which I used deception but not force. I have never attempted anything I did not accomplish."*

Critchley asked that Ellen should be allowed to change out of the clothes which had been bought in Calais, but by then she was so afraid of being again duped by Wakefield that she would not go into another room unaccompanied. Robert Turner had gone with her. The police then questioned her in French and allowed her to return to England.

Critchley had taken Ellen to the Hotel Meurice leaving Robert Turner and Grimsditch to finish their dealings with Wakefield.

That concluded the prosecution's evidence with which Wakefield had no argument. Grimsditch, in a long and detailed submission, asked the magistrates to commit Wakefield for trial on the charge of felony, quoting numerous statutes in particular that of Henry V11. He added that, in the previous case against William Wakefield, the only counter argument had been that Ellen was not heir apparent but only heir presumptive which would make the offence a misdemeanour. He also requested that Wakefield should not be given bail because of the severity of the crime - *"...this gross outrage against the peace of* (Mr Turner's) *family."*

Grimsditch's plea was not just lengthy, it was impassioned. The magistrates obviously appreciated his efforts for Mr Humphreys remarked, with a smile, that it had been a good speech for a jury. The court was cleared and the magistrates conferred for a full hour. Wakefield and Dr Davies spent the time walking on the green but the reporter commented that the high spirits of the accused were no longer apparent.

It fell to Mr Tatton to announce the verdict,

"Mr Edward Gibbon Wakefield, we have given full consideration to the nature of the charge exhibited against you, and the case has been fully and ably discussed by several gentlemen. The result of our deliberation is, that we feel ourselves bound to commit you.........for felony, and you therefore stand committed to take your trial at the ensuing Assizes for the county of Lancaster."

But Grimsditch had not finished. He wished to correct a misunderstanding by the public. He cited the article in "John Bull" which had been written by Wakefield, in which he had said he would surrender himself but that the Turner faction had not made arrangements. Grimsditch was in mid-sentence saying that, on the contrary, he had immediately accepted this offer of surrender when Mr Humphreys stated that this was not relevant and that Wakefield already had enough to oppress his mind. Grimsditch tried again. Wakefield responded,

"May I say a word or two? I have not put any statement in the "John Bull", nor any other newspaper. This is all I think it necessary to say in reply to Mr Grimsditch's remarks. I will stop here."

Grimsditch asserted that the statement with Wakefield's name on it had appeared but the threatened contretemps was averted by Mr

Newton deferring the argument. The witnesses were bailed to appear at the assizes and the case concluded.

The onlookers had had three and three quarter hours of entertainment. For those not present the reporter finished with his description of the accused,

> *"Mr Wakefield, we understand, is just turned thirty years of age. He is a genteel looking young man, about 5ft. 9 in. high, with light complexion, and is a juvenile likeness of the copper-plate engravings of Sir Walter Scott.*

The following day Edward Gibbon Wakefield was taken to Lancaster. Would there be a period of calm before the August Assizes? Not when Wakefield had a cause to pursue!

Grimsditch plays Detective

The mysterious article in "John Bull" continued to be a source of much speculation. In the same edition which covered the hearing at Disley, the "Courier" fuelled the debate,

> *"The long flippant narrative of the latest outrage which appeared in the last John Bull, is, as we hoped for Mr Wakefield's sake, formally disowned by him. It was at one time our intention to publish this lengthy detail of cold-blooded atrocity, but as it is now denounced as an unauthorised publication we will not pollute public morals and public decency by further advertising it".[1]*

It seems that, despite the "Courier's" best efforts to bury the article, it continued to excite the public imagination. By the next issue they were clearly doubting Wakefield's denial of authorship.

> *"We should think nobody but himself could have detailed the proceedings so minutely.....nobody else would go to the expense of publishing it......how greatly does it aggravate the monstrous offence! What must the moral part of the public of England think of the heart of that man, who, after despoiling an affectionate father of his daughter, turns into personal ridicule the affliction of the most disconsolate parent! Let Mr Wakefield ruminate on these matters in the gaol of Lancaster; and let those in this neighbourhood who have aided, comforted and abetted him in the circulation of his infamous memoir, chuckle over the fiendish fun they have ineffectually attempted to create, amidst the execrations of all classes of society."[2]*

The article proved so popular that it was brought out as a pamphlet and was put into circulation all over England. By whom? Thomas Grimsditch was hot on the trail. He visited the printer, a Mr Molineux in his premises at Fetter Lane in London, who told him that the order had come from James Garrod who worked as a clerk in a

---

[1] "Macclesfield Courier" 27 / 5 / 1826

[2] "Macclesfield Courier" 3 / 6 / 1826

Thomas Grimsditch
Reproduced with permission from Miss H Grimsditch, a descendant

barrister's chambers. The barrister was called Daniel Wakefield, brother of Edward senior and uncle of the abductors. Garrod stated that he had acted on the orders of Edward Gibbon Wakefield.

The next day Grimsditch returned to put more questions to the printer. This time he was in luck indeed, for Molineux produced a hand written copy of the pamphlet and a letter written by E G Wakefield indemnifying the printer from the consequences of having printed it. The handwriting in the two documents was identical. The printer also said he had instructions to send a copy to William Turner at Shrigley by the Manchester Mail.

Thus Grimsditch had evidence to prove that Wakefield was the author of the piece and that he had already lied in a court at the Rams Head. But he had another point to make. It was being argued that an article about the pamphlet, which had appeared in the "Courier", was prejudicial to the case. But he pointed out that it was another publication, the "Macclesfield Herald", in which the article had been printed, the "Courier" had merely commented on this. So the paper of which he was a proprietor was innocent of any prejudicial reporting.

That cleared up a technicality but what about the "Herald's" report influencing a jury? Grimsditch answered that too by pointing out the distance between Macclesfield and the trial town was over seventy miles, so the jury were highly unlikely to have read the report.

Grimsditch certainly had not let the grass grow under his feet, for he had also made great efforts to try to track down Edward Thevenot, Wakefield's servant and the man who had actually carried out the abduction. The servant had disappeared into France, probably to Wakefield's Paris home. Despite appeals to the French government and to the police authorities there, he could not be found and brought to Lancaster to answer the charges against him.

The court at the assizes heard Grimsditch's sworn affidavits before the trial started. Thus far so good. But not for long. The lawyers for the Wakefields took full advantage of every loophole they could find. The Turner family must have wondered if they would ever be free of their son-in-law.

The Summer Assizes

The assizes were scheduled for August. At the beginning of July the
Manchester Coach office foresaw the huge interest and an opportunity it
ought not to miss - it increased the fare to Lancaster from twelve to
twenty one shillings. All but the best beds in the town were already
booked at a guinea each, an unusually high cost. But then there were
upwards of a thousand witnesses to be housed, ninety five for
Wakefield's defence according to some papers, so beds were bound to
be in short supply. Morning and evening newspapers were ready to
compete to have the first reports. No expense was spared as they
stationed relays of horses along the route from Lancaster to London.
Nationally there was certainly huge interest, which had been whipped up
by the press, in events in Lancaster.

      Meanwhile in prison, the abductor, though reportedly not in his
usual high spirits, had his own apartments amid conditions as pleasant as
could be expected for one under arrest. Conditions in the gaol had been
considerably improved thirty years before by the building of quarters for
the inmates. Reporters tried to see him at every opportunity

> *"Mr W. takes daily as much exercise in the space allotted to him in
> the Castle of Lancaster as its narrow limits will allow. We saw
> him...perambulating the confined yard attached to his
> apartments....He is a genteel-looking man, of a rather slender make,
> and his knees incline forwards. He was dressed in a straw hat, blue
> surcoat and trowsers of the same colour. ....Perceiving that he was
> observed, he disappeared for a few minutes, ...soon afterwards,
> accompanied by a fashionably dressed lady, who hung upon his arm,
> he re-crossed the yard, and holding a letter in his hand, which he
> appeared to be reading, ascended the stairs to his apartment."[1]*

The preliminaries took place on Saturday, August 12th. The
Grand Jury reviewed the case. It was their duty to decide which of the

---

[1] Macclesfield Courier" 19 / 8 / 1826

Edward Gibbon Wakefield   Original drawing by A.Wivell 1823
Engraving by B Holl 1826
Reproduced by kind permission of the Alexander Turnbull Library, National Library
of New Zealand, Te Puna Matauranga o Aotearoa. Ref. A-042-023

charges the accused persons should answer. Early in the morning Turner brought his daughter to give her account. She was in a small court room for an hour and in the meantime a curious crowd outside were anxious to see Wakefield's young victim. Annoyingly for them, the Turners were determined that Ellen should not be subject to such attention. Four identically dressed young ladies emerged and walked, pursued by a baffled crowd, to the family's lodgings. The crowd was none the wiser, as they had no idea which of the heavily veiled quartet was Ellen.

Seemingly all was going well for the Turners. The Grand Jury came into the main court at six to present their bills. Their decision was that Edward Gibbon Wakefield and his brother William should stand trial for a misdemeanour, and that they should also face a charge of conspiracy, together with Thevenot and Frances Wakefield. No charges were to be brought against Edward Wakefield senior. So it was a case of misdemeanour, not one of felony. How the defence lawyers must have laughed up their sleeves and how they must have worked that weekend. They were really going to give the prosecution a fight on every tiny detail they could possible use. And of course they were going to earn themselves some enormous fees! The press foresaw even more interest and the public looked forward to excellent entertainment.

The court started proceedings at eight o'clock on the Monday with another case. But rumours of a motion to postpone the case against William had been rife and it was thought that motion might precede the scheduled sitting. This meant there was an unusual number of the public, jostling for places, and of members of the legal profession crammed round their table. The judge complained throughout the day of the noise and confusion in the court preventing it from doing its normal business. He was having none of the proposal to hear the motion before the planned case, it would have to wait until the end of the court's usual sitting.

It was five o'clock before Mr Scarlett could start his argument to have the case postponed. He had one idea of the law, the judge had another. The accused were not in court. The judge demanded their presence to enter a plea. Scarlett protested, but the judge prevailed and William and Edward Gibbon Wakefield were brought into the dock. For Mr Scarlett this too was wrong. William was on bail and had no business being in the dock. More argument ensued and eventually

William climbed over the front of the dock and wedged himself between barristers at their crowded table.

The court attempted to deal with Edward Gibbon first. He was charged with a misdemeanour, but was in custody for a felony. Scarlett maintained that the case should be postponed to the next assize in order that he should have time to prepare his case against this new charge, that he should not enter a plea until the next assize and that, since it was a less serious charge, he should also receive bail. The judge accepted that the case should be postponed but insisted that he should plead. Edward Gibbon Wakefield pleaded not guilty.

Then it was William's turn. Try as he might Scarlett could not influence the judge to change his opinion. The Grand Jury had brought in the same charge as the hearing at the Court of King's Bench which had released William on bail. Scarlett maintained that, if the two brothers were tried separately, months apart, for the same offence, the first trial would be prejudicial to the second, the same witnesses would be called at great expense and that, if the first defendant was found guilty and the second innocent, justice would not be served. Great was the confusion. But the judge was unmoved, William should enter a plea and come to trial in the next few days. He pleaded not guilty.

Frances too pleaded not guilty. Then there was the bail to be decided. William already had sureties of £500 from Dr Davies and £1,500 from a Mr Cuthbert who lived near Broadstairs in Kent. Edward Gibbon put up £2,500 himself, his Uncle Daniel, the barrister, and Dr Davies each put up £1,250. Frances' bail consisted of £2,000 from her husband and £1,000 each from her father and Daniel, her brother-in-law. Edward Gibbon's conditions also included a clause that he should keep the peace towards Mr Turner and his family. That same Monday evening he was released from the prison.

The case against William and Frances was to be heard on the following Monday, August 21st at 9.30 a.m. All precautions had been taken to deal with the expected stampede for places in the court. A report in the Lancaster Gazette, quoting a Manchester paper, described the scene,

> "....the Grand Jury box and the Ladies' Gallery presented the appearance of large beds of lilies, roses and tulips, thickly planted, and curiosity sparkled amongst them like the morning dew."[2]

2 "Lancaster Gazette." 2 / 9 / 1826

But rumours abounded that events would not be quite as planned.

Mr Justice Park made his entry but the barristers' table was remarkably deserted. Mr Brougham rose to ask that William Wakefield should appear. The judge agreed and the clerk called three times for William Wakefield to, *"...come forth, save you and your bail, or you will forfeit your recognizances."* And nothing happened - William had fled! All that was left for Brougham, the prosecutor, to do was to ensure that Dr Davies and Mr Cuthbert should be made to pay up, having failed to ensure William's appearance, and to ask for an arrest warrant for the fugitive.

Even here the Turners were thwarted. The judge could grant a warrant but it was only valid for Lancashire, application had to be made to the Court of King's Bench if the warrant was to cover the whole kingdom. Most of the witnesses had already gone home for it was well known that William had absconded.

It would all have to wait for the next assize! What an anti-climax for the public and the press.

The Evil Day Postponed

The "Courier" was exasperated by the whole affair,

> *"The result has not surprised us, although it has woefully
> disappointed the public. The moment we heard that the principal
> offender had been let out on bail…..we were prepared to expect that
> every species of trick, contrivance and chicanery would be resorted
> to by these Heroes of Abduction, to put off the "evil day"……….it
> would be idle to suppose that a man who is said to have acted so
> daring a part in a conspiracy the most foul and nefarious that ever
> disgraced the annals of this country, would hesitate to sacrifice the
> bail who had rescued him from the walls of a prison………..The "evil
> day" must and will eventually overtake them ……Mr Turner will
> never cease, til he has brought the whole gang to justice…..He feels
> that he has an indispensable duty to perform to society - that his
> cause is the cause of the public; and regardless of expense and
> inconvenience to himself, he will proceed steadily onward til every
> party……shall be brought…….to answer for this unparalleled
> outrage. …..The recognizances of William Wakefield, Mr Cuthbert
> and Dr Davies have already been estreated…….William Wakefield….
> is said to have fled to France……"The British Traveller" broadly
> asserts that "the whole covey have taken flight"….and that the two
> brothers are not expected to return……….the consequences would
> be…..the forfeit…..of £13,000 and would operate as a complete
> banishment, which is perhaps the best riddance of the crew. This
> case….shows the soundness of the discretion exercised by the
> committing Magistrates, in refusing bail for both brothers, and
> thereby preventing their escape from the hands of justice."[1]*

The "Lancaster Gazette" expressed the same sentiments,

> *"…all the knowing ones were prepared…they saw enough of bye
> play, jockeyship, restiveness, and shying of the Judge's chair, to
> indicate a very indifferent contest. Considerable disappointment was*

---

[1] "Macclesfield Courier" 26 / 8 /1826

*felt,...particularly the more confiding sex, who waited impatiently to
see and hear, in a suffocating crowd, what they might rely upon
reading leisurely at home in a few days....we are sorry...that the
course of justice should be stayed...in an affair of such importance to
the peace of society, the security of property, and the character of
English jurisprudence....It may be unreasonable to expect that a
swindler who decoys a young lady from her family and friends, for
the sake of her fortune, should be punished in a summary a way as
the poachers, who wire hares, or should be hanged like a horse-
dealer - the age of chivalry is too far gone. ...Among the
multitudinous annual shoals of statutes...none... can be found of a
later date than the reign of Philip and Mary....that attempt to provide
an adequate punishment for the abstraction of such a chattel as an
only daughter.....In England the rite of marriage is performed within
the walls of a church......But we live within the smell of a religion,
where any boy of fourteen and any girl of twelve may, at any time of
the day or night, be united by a reverend blacksmith, whose boast is,
that when trade is good, he can get regularly drunk three times in
four and twenty hours.....it remains to be tried whether the
perpetrators of so flagitious an outrage can escape unpunished in a
country which boasts that no one is beyond the reach of its laws."*[2]

In the same edition Daniel Wakefield was reported to have said
that William had fled, with the blessing of his family, in order to ensure a
joint trial. He promised that the family would compensate Dr Davies and
Mr Cuthbert. In fact the legalities failed in this too. It was reported that
bailiffs had seized goods from Mr Cuthbert but it seems to have been
agreed, that as long as William came to be tried with his brother, the bail
would not be forfeited and any losses would be made up by the courts
because of a mistake they made.

After that the coverage of the Wakefields' activities became
more intermittent. There were reports that the Wakefields' grandfather,
Priscilla's husband, had died at an advanced age. There were also a few
details of a case, concerning a disparity in the handling of money
belonging to Mrs Pattle, which involved Edward senior in his role as a
trustee.

But in September there was a flurry of speculation caused by
another report in "John Bull". The earlier article had been proved
correct, so was this, with its mis-spelt names and places, just scurrilous
speculation?

---

[2] "Lancaster Gazette 26 / 8 / 1826

*"We understand that Mr Leigh of Lynn, near Macclesfield, who
possesses immense estates in Cheshire, which lie contiguous to those
of Mr Turner of Shrigley Park, was on the point of paying his
addresses to Miss Turner, when she was carried off by Mr Wakefield.
The circumstances we understand put a stop to the preliminaries of
so advantageous an alliance as regards property, and upon the result
of the trial of Mr Wakefield depends whether Mr Leigh's hand and
estates shall be joined with the hand and estates of Miss Turner."[3]*

The "Courier" was dismissive, describing the article as silly and devoid
of truth.

In early October the "Courier" reported that Edward Gibbon
Wakefield had been on a visit to Dr Davies. Later there were rumours
that he had been seen frequenting the lanes of Cheshire close to
Shrigley. William seems to have stayed in France, safe from being taken
into custody in England for absconding.

Wakefield was still determined to prove the marriage legal and
what could be more natural than a Christmas present from a husband to
his wife? The "Times" reported that Ellen had received a newly
published book of poems called "Forget Me Not". It came in a parcel
delivered by coach and at first sight there was nothing to reveal who the
sender was. But inside there was a drawing of the would-be husband
and a translation of a poem called "The praise of love". "The Times"
quotes the last lines

*"Let others deem time must unloose
Love's finest bonds, decay'd by use,
Or when those bonds we cherish:
For me, whatever be my lot,
I still will love - when I do not,
Why let me die and perish."[4]*

It was reported that a highly indignant Ellen, wanted to send the present
back but that the ever calm Grimsditch advised that the book be
ignored. In any case Ellen could enjoy the poems because her father had
given her a copy a few days earlier.

Just a month before the case was due to be heard at the spring
assizes in Lancaster, Wakefield's lawyers tried another tack. They
appealed to the Court of King's Bench to have the case tried there in
front of a special jury and more than one judge. Their argument was
that, because there were so many points of law to be decided, a single

---

[3] "John Bull" 18 / 9 / 1826
[4] "The Times" 23 / 3 / 1827

judge might be unable to give all the rulings. This would mean he would be forced to postpone proceedings to take advice, an action which would incur even more expense. Their second option was to move the case to Carlisle or York, where the potential jurors would not have been swayed by the adverse comments of the press. They rebutted the claim that Wakefield himself had attempted to influence public opinion by writing to the press saying that he had only answered his critics, he had not started the press speculation.

The court listened and debated but found against the Wakefields, so the case was due to be heard at Lancaster at the end of March, 1827.

The Trial

Once more preparations were made. The press was out in force, sightseers crammed into the city, witnesses and members of the legal profession had to be accommodated. Surely this time, a year after the abduction, the case had to be heard. It was due to start on Thursday, 22nd March.

On the Wednesday it became obvious that Mr Scarlett, who was to lead for the defence, was suffering from an exceptionally heavy cold. The judge gave him a day's grace to recover, the case would be heard on Friday. The press reported that Mr Scarlett was decidedly off colour as he pleaded his cause, but at long last the Wakefields were to be tried.

By five in the morning the crowds had started to form on the hill round the castle. The authorities had anticipated the interest and Mr Gibson, the High Sheriff, had even had the forethought to issue tickets for the public gallery to his friends, many being elegantly dressed ladies. Before seven o'clock they were allowed into the splendid new Shire Hall through a private entrance. Some of the ladies were actually allowed to sit on the bench with the judge, other members of the public were seated in the special jury box.

All the members of the press who wished to hear the proceedings were also admitted, though many were then ousted when it was realised room had to be found for the numerous lawyers who were present. Many reporters had been promised bonuses for being the first to file their stories, so the uproar this caused can well be imagined. Barriers were erected and javelin men lined the passage into the court so that witnesses and barristers could enter.

The judge, Mr Baron Hullock, made his entrance at eight ready to try some minor cases, but these were postponed and by eight thirty everything was ready for the great event. Mr Turner entered. Members of his family were in the box to the judge's left facing the jury. Mr Turner himself sat next to Cross, the leading prosecutor. Mrs Turner was not well enough to attend. Edward Gibbon Wakefield, his father and uncle and their lawyers came in and sat at the bar. Mr Higgin the Governor of the castle was then ordered to bring in William from the cells to which he had been confined for debt concerning his bail.

More commotion ensued at the appearance of the lawyers with a huge number of documents for which they found there was insufficient room. Then ten merchants, mainly from Manchester and Liverpool, and two gentlemen were sworn in as jurors and the case proper started.

There are three images of the trial, the work of a lawyer who was present, in the care of Lancashire County Council at the Castle. A pencil sketch of the lawyers with a key to their identities is dated 1826, which would make it a record of the previous abortive hearing in August. One is a watercolour, presumably the next to be painted. The third is in oils. But the second and third differ slightly in the people they portray. The sketch adds further confusion because the names of the lawyers do not exactly coincide with the lawyers present at any one of the hearings. Was the artist amalgamating all the hearings to make an overall representation? Whatever his intentions, his work certainly gives a marvellous impression of the packed Shire Hall and how intimidating it must have been for most of the witnesses to give their evidence.

The indictments were read by Mr Starkie. The first was for conspiracy, the second abduction for lucre and gain, the third was for a felony and there were other similar counts. Mr Sergeant Cross opened for the prosecution by praising the previous Attorney-General, who would have been prosecuting, had he not been promoted. Then he recited the facts of the case as the prosecution saw them. His speech was long and detailed, he missed no opportunity to stress the wickedness of the deed. He presented letters between the Wakefields, letters from Frances, the letter which fooled the Daulbys. Nothing was left out.

Eventually he started examining the witnesses, the first being William Turner who was followed by Elizabeth Daulby. She, though unwell, gave her account clearly. Scarlett, for the defence, questioned her about Ellen. Miss Daulby described her as well-grounded and sagacious. At this point Brougham stepped in and elicited a further opinion that Ellen was trusting and confiding. So the postboys, chambermaids, and innkeepers were called and examined and told the story of the abduction and the marriage. Grimsditch's evidence took the longest time, for it was crucial to the case. At last Cross called Ellen who was accompanied into court by her Aunt Ellen. The spectators got their first whiff of excitement.

The "Courier" gave a short description of Ellen,

"She was plainly dressed in black silk, and a narrow straw bonnet trimmed with red riband - but the style was genteel. The upper part of her person, not being covered with a shawl, exhibited a most graceful figure. For her age she is rather tall, but not above the height which good figures are generally. - Her lady-like manner, her intelligence and firmness during her examination, attracted the attention of the court, so as to induce all around us to join in admiration of the manner in which she conducted herself. She answered every question with a precision and correctness of language which showed her education had been strictly attended to." [1]

Wakefield, holding his sketching pencil in his mouth, gazed at her as she gave her evidence. Ellen disregarded him.

Before she could be sworn Scarlett was on his feet objecting and she had to retire while the legal arguments raged. Scarlett maintained that he proposed to show the marriage was legal in which case Ellen could not testify against her husband. All the old arguments were advanced, but this time Brougham prevailed on the judge to exercise his discretion on the behalf of the prosecution. The case proceeded and Ellen took the oath.

Her evidence was quite straightforward. Throughout the emphasis was on the fact that she had been deceived into agreeing to the marriage. Scarlett's cross-examination was only about the ring which had proved too large, another had been bought in Calais. The letter which Ellen had written from Calais was also mentioned and this caused more questioning from the prosecution to make sure the jury realised that Ellen had written it at the dictation of Wakefield.

Ellen's ordeal was now over and there only remained her Uncle Henry's evidence to be heard before the case for the defence commenced. By now it was obvious to the court that the defence was not going to oppose the facts which the prosecution had presented to the jury. Wakefield had been exposed as a heartless villain who had abducted an under-age girl he had never seen in order to obtain her

---

[1] "Macclesfield Courier" 31 / 3 / 1827 which is also the source of all the quotations in this chapter.

fortune. This much was undisputed, the spectators had their hate figure, could they look forward to some fun at his expense?

Mr Scarlett addressed the jury. He also took the opportunity to extol the virtues of the ex-Attorney General before opening the defence by stating that he could never defend what Wakefield had done. It was wrong. But Wakefield was entitled to justice, not the revenge which Mr Turner was seeking. The case against Frances Wakefield, he submitted, should not have been brought for it was impossible to prove she had been guilty of a crime. Then he attempted to prove that Ellen had been a willing participant. She could have gone to her uncle's house from the Albion Hotel and she did not appear frightened or coerced at any point. After continuing in this vein for quite some time he concluded his opening statement, saying that his intention was to show the marriage was legal.

The judge confessed that he thought Mr Scarlett's defence did not answer the charges before the court and that he thought the prosecution had already proved their point. But he allowed Scarlett to continue by calling his witnesses. They had had nothing to do for some hours. When they eventually gave their evidence, it became apparent that many of them had spent some of the time drinking - it all added to the spectator sport that the case had become after so much publicity. The papers reported laughter in court throughout the defence evidence. The judge's reported interjections did nothing to calm or quieten the situation, he seemed to be enjoying the spectacle too!

Ann Bradley from the Devonshire Arms told the court that she had taken gingerbread to Ellen who did not seem dispirited. Mr Sergeant Cross and the rest of the prosecution team seemed to relax and to take part in the courtroom banter. The one question they posed to the "good woman" was whether the gingerbread was good. By this means they continually ridiculed the defence's case.

Sarah Coleman from the Rose and Crown at Kirby Lonsdale found herself being led on by combined tactics. As she was cross-examined she agreed that Ellen had been cheerful like a girl going home from school to see her parents. Scarlett countered, for this was not the form of words to help his case, and suggested she appeared like a girl going to her wedding. Cross then asked if young ladies going to be married were cheerful. Sarah thought marriage was a serious business.

Brougham added the punch line by commenting that he assumed she was not married.[2]

It was the evidence of David Laing, who had conducted the marriage ceremony, which was to "top the bill" for the public, but which was so crucial for the both the prosecution and the defence. The "Macclesfield Courier" described him for their readers,

> *"In appearance this old man was made to assume a superiority over his usual companions. Somebody had dressed him in a black coat, and velvet waistcoat, with a shining pair of topboots - the shape of his hat, too, resembled the clerical fashion. He seemed a vulgar fellow, though not without shrewdness and that air of familiarity......he leaned forward towards the counsel....with a ludicrous expression of gravity......and answered every answer with a knitting of his wrinkled brow, and significant nodding of his head, which gave peculiar force to his quaintness of phraseology and occasionally convulsed the court with laughter."*

It was Brougham who cross-examined with the aim of ridiculing the marriage. He questioned Laing about his past life and how he came to perform the ceremonies. When Laing said he had been a merchant Brougham defined this as being a travelling vagrant pedlar. But Laing would not be persuaded to deny the validity of his marriages as opposed to those carried out by the Scottish clergy.

The judge was fast losing patience with the defence case,

> *"...is it by a fellow like this, that you mean to prove the custom of the law of Scotland as to valid marriage! Show me by proper authority how a marriage got up as this has been can be valid anywhere. This you must show......But we are not to ramble all day with witnesses of this description. Do not take us from Gretna to Calais with witnesses who really can prove nothing. I so trust to your discretion in the use of the time of the court."*

After examining Quillac, who gave his evidence through an interpreter, Scarlett played his trump card with his last witness, Mr MacNeil. He was called as an expert on Scottish law and stated that the marriage was indeed valid. MacNeil, under Brougham's cross-examination, admitted that he considered the marriage to be invalid if force had been used but valid if only deceit had induced Ellen to consent. The legal argument grew complicated on both sides.

---

[2] Brougham's participation in the trial is interesting. He married in secret in Scotland in 1819. In 1856 he steered a Marriage Act through Parliament.

Eventually Brougham asked whether a marriage performed by a drunken pedlar, in an alehouse, before a postboy was legal. MacNeil still thought such a marriage would be legal.

Baron Hullock intervened by asking MacNeil if he knew of a case like this before in Scotland. MacNeil said he knew of no such case. It was enough for the judge. He told Scarlett that he had decided that Ellen's testimony could be used by the jury to assist them in bringing in a verdict.

Cross now summed up for the prosecution. His indignation at the bare-faced villainy of the accused grew as he addressed the jury. Not only had they committed an atrocious act, they had aggravated it in the court.

It was eight o'clock before Baron Hullock started to address the jury. He had only said a very few sentences when the jury told him they already knew what verdict they would reach. The lawyers conferred and the charge of using force was dropped. The jury retired to decide on their decision regarding Frances Wakefield. They took a mere twenty minutes to find all three defendants guilty on the charge of conspiracy and the public made it plain they thoroughly agreed.

By now it was late and the prosecution requested an adjournment until the following morning, when the other charges were to be decided. The court rose at half past nine.

Throughout the long day everyone present was engrossed in the proceedings, even if their motives were very different. But all had one thing in common. No one present had heard a huge explosion which had shaken the whole of that part of the north-west coast. It was thought at first to be an earthquake. In fact a vessel carrying gunpowder and cotton had caught fire and the crew abandoned ship before it was blown out of the water and disintegrated completely. The people in the Shire Hall were so engrossed they failed to notice it.

What a day!

The Trial 1826

Reproduced by kind permission of Lancashire County Council

Brougham is standing, his arm over Scarlett's head, Cross is second from the left on the front rank

The Trial 1826

Reproduced by kind permission of Lancashire County Council

Shrigley Hall Hotel, Golf & Country Club   © Toadstone Design   Reproduced with permission

KMA

Gretna Hall Hotel

Rams Head, Disley

KMA

Just Deserts

The following morning the court was again crowded, but the spectacle was not to be repeated. Scarlett knew he was beaten and submitted a plea of guilty to one other count. He understood this would be enough to satisfy the prosecution. The Prothonotary ordered the jury to bring in a guilty verdict because of an agreement between the parties. This form of words was too much for Mr Sergeant Cross, he was incensed. There had been no agreement, the prosecution was quite willing to present their case on all the charges. Mr Scarlett hastily confirmed that there had been no arrangement and Cross was appeased. As long as the verdict was guilty to whatever charges the judge was now asked to consider, he and his client would be satisfied.

At last it was over, and the two brothers were confined in the castle at Lancaster until sentenced at the Court of King's Bench. Frances, however, was deemed to have been punished enough by being found guilty and was allowed her freedom.

The press thought they could squeeze more out from the affair. They advertised books of the trial including all the documents which had been cited. Many of the papers published verbatim accounts of the trial - "The Times" brought out a special edition. The editorials poured condemnation on the abductor and his accomplices.

The "Macclesfield Courier"[1] thoughtfully gave its readers a selection from the London press. The "Sunday Times" had compared Wakefield to a Tartar

> "*who tears a Georgian maid from the arms of her weeping parents...It is only astonishing that the law of England still tolerates such a mockery as the Gretna-green ceremony, by a pedlar.*"

---

[1] "Macclesfield Courier" 7 / 4 / 1827

"The Times" averred that

> *"The act of the Wakefields forms an era in the history of crime......an*
> *act...never known to occur till now in the history of civilized*
> *man....."*

"The Age" commented on the peculiar depravity of the abductor
and continued

> *"Unless some legal interposition is placed between society at large,*
> *and the ungovernable desires or ambition of such unworthy members*
> *of it, our private thresholds are no longer secure.... in addition to the*
> *most replenished knave, we consider him to be about the greatest*
> *fool, we have ever had the misfortune to encounter."*

"The Watchman" advocated a marriage act to cover the whole
of the kingdom, for

> *"The fact that a fellow can inveigle a poor girl across an imaginary*
> *border, and then, by making her repeat some mumbling ceremony*
> *before a drunken blacksmith, have it in his power to claim her as his*
> *wife, is so monstrous a piece of absurdity, that it ought not to be*
> *tolerated one moment."*

"The Atlas" could not remember an offence more odious and
castigated the villain for his

> *"insinuation calculated to blast the future prospects of the individual,*
> *who had already suffered by the machinations of the conspirators".*

It was nearly eight weeks before the brothers came up for
sentencing in London. Again virtually verbatim reports were published
by several papers. But the really striking feature is that, though the
prosecution case was conducted by the same leading members of the
legal profession, this time Edward Gibbon Wakefield presented his own
case. Whether this was his choice or whether he was constrained by his
financial situation is not certain and of course he did have an uncle who
was a barrister. But he did attempt to win the sympathy of the court by
pointing out how much the case had cost him to defend.

The facts of the case were restated and Cross asked for a
sentence on the conspiracy charge. Wakefield then presented an
affidavit. Once more he brought up the fact that he had been sent for
trial on a felony. He had spent £3000 in preparing his defence on this
charge and had had to sell a life annuity for £1,500. When he had
appeared for trial, the charge had been altered which had resulted in
more expenditure. He had spent over four months in prison. Then he
tried to save his brother from severe punishment. He stated that William

had been far more concerned with his own marriage and had only acted under direction.

William's affidavit was then considered. He too said he had acted under his brother's direction and that as a consequence of the trial his wife had had no settlement from her father and that the couple's only source of income came in the form of voluntary funding from their fathers. He had absconded to prevent separate trials but had no intention of avoiding a joint trial.

The Attorney-General appeared for William only. He refused to justify the crime in any way but he did point out the difference between the crimes of the two brothers. He merely asked for a degree of mercy to be shown to his client.

Now it was the turn of the abductor himself. In a written statement he asked the court for justice, not vengeance, and cited other cases which he maintained were similar. He accused Cross of wilful mis-statement and maintained that the charge of fraud upon his wife had not been fairly tried, but that it was possible that it might in the future be tried more fairly in the House of Lords.

Then came the bombshell. He referred to his wife being allowed to give evidence against him. Dramatically he paused to allow the prosecution to object to his raising a matter of great repugnance. No objection was forthcoming. He continued, implying that Ellen's evidence contradicted the assurance, which he had given, that the marriage had not been consummated. But, he said, he had not put his wife into the witness box, that was the doing of the prosecution, so they must take the blame for

> *"the introduction of which every man of delicacy or proper feeling must regret."*[2]

He considered that his lack of questioning on this subject was to his credit.

> *"He would rather had suffered himself to be apostrophised as a wretch by the learned Sergeant, than have hurt the feelings of the unhappy person whose interests were sacrificed in the blind pursuit of vengeance upon him."*

His final ploy for leniency was to say he would not draw on his children's legacy from their mother if he was fined, but would suffer the imprisonment for non-payment.

---

[2] "Macclesfield Courier" 19 / 5 / 1827 which is also the source of the subsequent quotations in this chapter.

Cross, Williams and Brougham then addressed the court. All three took up the insinuation, which Wakefield had just introduced, and demolished it. Wakefield had written to his brother repeating the statement that the marriage had not been consummated. This had been a voluntary statement of fact and the letter had been produced during the course of the trial. The abductor, they argued, had thus aggravated the original offence, either by committing perjury, or by trying to injure Ellen's character in order to blight the rest of her life and that of her grief-stricken parents. Brougham waxed lyrical,

> *"that address* (Wakefield's) *was not dictated by the feelings of the moment; it had been seriously prepared and concocted in the retirement of gaol; it betrayed the same crafty spirit which pervaded the whole conduct of him in whose sordid machinations the crime was originally hatched; it betrayed the same malignity, the cold-blooded disregard for the feelings of others, the same mighty contempt of the law, the same utter disregard of facts which had characterised the whole proceeding......Miss Turner's honour stood unimpeached. All the evidence supported that fact. It was the only consolation which her afflicted and venerable parents would carry with them from the Court, with the exception of that which their Lordships would award as the consummation of laborious, disinterested, and painful efforts, made, not solely for the prosecutor's own sake, but for the sake of all the parents in the kingdom, and for the vindication of outraged law."*

Mr Justice Bayley announced the sentence. He described the crime as

> *"a conspiracy of a more aggravated description, and from baser motives, I can hardly conceive to have entered into the mind of man."*

Both Wakefields were to serve three years, William in Lancaster, Edward Gibbon in Newgate.

Divorce

At long last the brothers were behind bars, but technically Ellen was Mrs Edward Gibbon Wakefield. William Turner still had a problem to resolve. The day after the sentencing, Lord Redesdale presented a petition to the House of Lords for permission to introduce a bill to declare the marriage null and void. It was an extraordinary event, his lordship had had to go back to 1691 to find a similar case. He recommended that a committee of the whole House should consider the situation. But their lordships were concerned as to the legality of the marriage in the first place. The Earl of Eldon wanted a decision on whether Miss Turner, if she was legally married, could give evidence against her husband. Would there first have to be an Act of Parliament to legalise such evidence? Turner must have despaired - these arguments had already been debated for hours in the courts, they were going round in circles. Thankfully the matter was referred to a committee which was to sit the following week.

Wakefield resorted to his pen yet again. If Eldon had argued for his side might not the peer be made use of to support his cause? He addressed a letter to Lord Eldon which, he said, contained his instructions at his trial to his counsel on cross-examining Ellen. This was evidence which had never been presented in court because it was intended to refute the charge of fraud, a charge which the judge had said had been proved by the very act of abduction. Wakefield had intended it to refute fraud by citing Ellen's reaction to him, not the seizure itself. He still sought to prove that the marriage had been contracted out of Ellen's love for him once the abduction had resulted in their meeting. A nice point on which Wakefield was determined to elaborate on appeal to the House of Lords.

The account in the letter expands on the article in "John Bull", the article which Grimsditch had proved to be written by Wakefield. He describes how, from their first meeting at the Albion Hotel, he had been very affectionate and tender towards her and she had responded. When he had caressed her she had received his caresses with evident satisfaction. She was delighted to be going to Gretna Green and had sat all night in the carriage with her head on his shoulder and his arm around her waist. She had spoken of her father's violent temper. When they were alone in the carriage they had done nothing but laugh and kiss. He pointed out that Ellen had given a totally different account to the jury, in other words that she had lied in court. There was also included the evidence from a valet at Quillac's hotel which implied that there had been free movement between the bedrooms at the hotel.

This was a last ditch attempt by Wakefield to prove the validity of the marriage and so force Turner to accept him as his son-in-law. Did he really expect to be believed when he had sworn that the marriage was not consummated and when he had written to his brother voluntarily saying the same thing? Did he think that he would be believed despite the feeling against him in the country?

The bill was allowed and had a rather curious second reading at the end of May. The "Courier" reported that the public's appetite for the case was as keen as ever and by early morning crowds had filled every avenue leading to the House of Lords. Several attempts were made to force the doors but they were defended by a party of constables whose duty was to admit only those with invitations. Both Wakefields were present as was Ellen and her father. They were to face packed benches inside the House for the peers were just as interested as the public outside. Proceedings started at ten thirty and dragged on until nearly five.

The first to speak was Mr Adams, the counsel for William Turner. He confessed that no precedent had been found for the case in either the records of the Lords or in the Ecclesiastical Courts. He asked the House to consider that Wakefield had married Ellen by force and fraud in order to gain her fortune. Ellen's free will had been annihilated, therefore the contract she had made was not valid. Once more the facts of the abduction were stated, then Adams turned to other cases of abduction. Witnesses were called starting with Ellen's father.

During all the evidence Edward Gibbon Wakefield took copious notes. In previous hearings he had sketched some of the witnesses, but then he had been represented, now he was on his own.

After Cross had examined Turner, the Lord Chancellor asked Wakefield if he wanted to cross-examine the witness. Wakefield pleaded that, though he was prepared to refute the allegations in the bill, he was totally unprepared for the hearing to take this form. The Lord Chancellor would have none of it, Wakefield would have the opportunity to state his case but Wakefield again protested that his witnesses were in Scotland and France and it was impossible to call them to the House immediately. He was given one more chance to put questions and, when that was refused, he was granted leave to retire. After a few moments of legal discussion he was recalled, but again refused to co-operate and was told that the investigation would go on whether he was there or not. Both Wakefields then left the Chamber with their prison escorts.

The investigation continued with evidence from Miss Daulby and then Ellen herself. She was attended by four other ladies. Her dress was of black silk and she wore a straw hat with no veil. By now she must have been used to speaking in public!

Eventually Cross summed up by contrasting the afflicted parent with the convicted imposter who had that day audaciously demanded as his lawful prize, the daughter of the afflicted parents. If their lordships refused the bill then

> *"this young lady.....would be obliged to go with her base betrayer, into that prison, where he was now suffering the punishment of his crime - to Newgate - and having remained there to finish her moral education for three years, in the society of such a man, she would come out into the world, the pure and innocent bride of a convicted and punished offender."* [1]

Now it was Wakefield's turn to argue that the marriage was legal and should not be dissolved. He stated that he had had no idea that the hearing would be open to witnesses. All he was expecting was to be heard on why he thought the consideration of the bill should be delayed, in other words until he had appealed to the Lords against his conviction. He again protested that he had not had chance to call any of his witnesses. He said the bill alleged he had used fraud, force, intimidation and threats against his wife. He had not been convicted of force, the charge of force had never been tried, therefore it should not be used in the bill. His witnesses had not been allowed to give their evidence on that point at his trial. He stated that it had cost him £8,000 to bring his witnesses twice to Lancaster.

---

[1] "Macclesfield Courier" 2 / 6 / 1827 which is the source of the subsequent quotations in this chapter.

He went on,

> *"I assert...that my wife married me through love and affection, and through those motives only."*

He then took quite some time to read, from one of the printed reports of the trial, the testimony of the witnesses who had sworn that Ellen was unrestrained and happy to be with Wakefield on the journey and after the marriage.

Lord Delamere interrupted to point out that Wakefield should be telling the Lords what his evidence would consist of, not reading the evidence of witnesses at the trial. Eldon countered by saying he had a right to read it and the right to challenge the fraud and force accusation to show why he should not have been convicted.

Wakefield was allowed to conclude his address and was taken out of the chamber. At this stage Grimsditch was recalled and assured the house that he had given Wakefield all the papers concerning this hearing ten days before.

The Lord Chancellor stated that, during the ten days Wakefield had had to start calling witnesses, he had made no attempt so to do. This provoked the peers into cries of hear, hear. The House saw an opportunity to demonstrate its feelings against the miscreant and added their agreement to each of the Lord Chancellor's points. Wakefield had not taken his chance to cross-examine. The case for the bill had been made. Wakefield, even if his witnesses had testified, could not have altered the evidence they had just heard. Cheers and hear hears became more frequent. The Lord Chancellor thought the bill should be brought forward with no more delays.

Eldon agreed. He had read the same printed pamphlet as the one Wakefield was quoting from and thought that it could not alter the case before them. He went on to note that once Miss Turner had been told of the deception practised on her she had refused to have anything to do with Wakefield. This produced loud cheering. Obviously Eldon had not been convinced by Wakefield's letter. The bill went forward to its third reading.

On leaving the Houses of Parliament Wakefield was hissed by the crowds. The "Courier" rejoiced,

> *"We cannot suppose that anything could have been so interesting as the laying bare one of the most abandoned, worthless reptiles that ever poisoned the earth by its blighting progress...a man, to whom*

Cain was an Angel of Light in the comparison, we most heartily express our joy, that a cold, heartless villain....has been CRUSHED."

The bill passed its third reading in the Lords on June 6th and went down to the Commons where it was introduced by Peel. His speech was cheered on at regular intervals. He stated that the main purpose of the bill was to prevent further injury to Mr Turner. No other remedy was available to the family. If they applied to the Ecclesiastical Courts it would take at least three years, even if Wakefield did not try to delay the eventual verdict. By that time Turner may be dead and his fortune would be at the disposal of the villain. Under these circumstances he thought it right that the House should give the relief which the Turner family sought. The House was in no doubt whatsoever, it agreed with every word. It requested the evidence which had been received by the Lords and the bill was accepted.

Its progress was now a formality. On June 14th the bill received the royal assent and Ellen was free of Wakefield at last.

Time to Rejoice

On the same day that the bill became law, William Turner travelled back home to Shrigley. He had spent at least £10,000 on the case but it had been well spent. His fortune, and that of his brother, was safe. Now all they had to do was to find a suitable husband for Ellen.

As he passed through Macclesfield, just a few miles from Shrigley, the bells of the churches were ringing in celebration. There were other events for Macclesfield folk to enjoy as well, for the famous Mr Green was demonstrating his hot air balloon by taking off from the Gas Works Yard. This was his seventy third flight, unfortunately the paper does not record how long a flight nor where he landed!

The following Saturday evening it was Ellen's turn to be greeted by bells.

> *"Nothing could exceed the gratification of the inhabitants of this town...at the happy restoration of Miss Turner to her family and friends. Cordial Congratulations. The bells of both our churches greeted her return. Villagers and tenantry assembled to welcome Miss Turner at Shrigley with bands, music and ringing of bells on her approach to the village about 8.00pm. She was received by the assembled crowd with the most joyous acclamations."* [1]

For the next few months the Turner family stayed out of the news. William's year as High Sheriff had long since finished so he could concentrate on his business affairs. It seems that Ellen did not return to school. But changes were certainly afoot.

However, let us catch up on changes in the lives of other characters in our tale. Two months before the trial, the Wakefield brothers gained a half-sister, the child of their father and Frances. She had been charged with them and had been found guilty but had escaped punishment. That child had just celebrated her first birthday when Dr

---

[1] "Macclesfield Courier" 23 / 6 / 1827

Davies, her grandfather, died. One wonders at the effect on him of the scandal involving his daughter because he was such a highly respected figure in Macclesfield and the surrounding area. Dr Davies' tomb is just inside the gate in the churchyard at Prestbury.

Frances and her husband went to Blois, where they are said to have established the silk industry. Irma O'Connor says that Frances and Edward senior remained estranged from Edward Gibbon for the next twenty years. This is contradicted in Earles' book on Macclesfield. [2] He states that the couple lived for many years at Great Oak Farm in Sutton near Macclesfield where Frances had inherited land from her mother. He also says that Edward Gibbon Wakefield wrote some of his best work there. When Frances died at Blois her remains were brought back and buried in the same grave as her father.

Two more deaths followed the trial. David Laing fell ill on his way home from Lancaster and never recovered. He died at the end of June 1827.

In the September "The Gentleman's Magazine" carried a sad notice,

> *"Aug.11. At Quiddenham, the seat of her uncle the Earl of Albermarle, Mrs Wakefield, only dau(ghter) of Sir John Sydney, bart., of Penshurst, and wife of Wm Wakefield, who was lately sentenced to twelve months imprisonment in Lancaster Castle, for aiding his brother in the abduction of Miss Turner. This accomplished and beautiful young lady has fallen victim to a broken heart. She has left one infant daughter, six months old"*

For the Daulbys the abduction of Ellen from their premises could have been disastrous. In fact the school continued to be patronised. Maybe prospective parents thought the sisters would be careful not to let the same thing happen again and that the benefits of such a good education outweighed the slight risk.

Having recorded what happened to some of our characters let us turn back to our principal concern, Ellen.

---

2 "Streets and Houses of Old Macclesfield" John Earles. M.T.D. Rigg Publications 1990

True Marriage

The church at Prestbury was busy in January 1828. On the 8th Thomas Legh's younger sister Margaret was married to Robert Dalziel. Just six days later on the 14th the wealthy owner of Lyme Park and next door neighbour to the Turners, Thomas Legh himself, was married there. His bride was Ellen. "John Bull" had been proved correct again! The wedding party made their way back to Shrigley to celebrate with a breakfast and then Mr and Mrs Thomas Legh went on to Lyme, Ellen's new home.

Thomas was thirty six and an exceedingly eligible man. It had even been rumoured that he had been considered for a peerage. His house at Lyme[1] had been remodelled recently by Lewis Wyatt, it was surrounded by a huge Park and an extensive area of farms and some industry. He had immense estates around St Helens and Newton le Willows. He owned the racecourse, which was then at Newton, and Haydock and Golborne Parks. His father had put these estates in jeopardy by not marrying and thereby having no legitimate heir. Thomas was only four and a half when his father died. It had taken many years of legal disputes before the estates were confirmed in law to be the property of his eldest recognised son. Thomas needed a legitimate heir to succeed to them on his death.

Ellen was seventeen. She was to inherit a vast fortune so it was imperative that she should make a good marriage and then produce an heir to inherit and control the businesses and the fortune. What could be better than a marriage between these two and an eventual amalgamation of the wealth of both families.

---

[1] Given to the National Trust in 1946 by Thomas' great, great nephew, Richard Legh, 3rd Lord Newton. It was Pemberley in the BBC's production of Jane Austen's "Pride and Prejudice".

How William and Jane Turner felt after nearly two years of anguish can only be imagined. At times they must have despaired of ever having their daughter restored to them. The legal processes were slow and sometimes the odds were stacked against them, seeming to favour the villain of the piece. Now they could put the past behind them and look forward to that first longed for grandchild. Ellen was only a few miles away, their son-in-law was well able to look after her and the family's fortune was now ensured.

And they were not the only ones to celebrate the big day. In Blackburn the "Mail" reported on the celebrations there,

> _"In consequence of this event, which took place at Prestbury on Monday a.m. about eight o'clock the bells of our parish church struck off a merry peal, and continued to ring at intervals throughout the whole of that day and yesterday. The people employed at the extensive print works at Mill Hill and Euwood near this Town, of the firm of Robert Turner & Co were indulged in a half day's holiday. In addition to this two fat beasts and twelve sheep were slaughtered and distributed in suitable proportions amongst those who have families, with each a quart of beer from the Hall. The single men and women had one shilling each allowed to regale themselves with, and the children, whose parents are not employed at the works, had sixpence each given to them. At Euwood one sheep was roasted whole, and another was boiled entire in a large copper used for other purposes, on the premises. The manager of the works, and their wives, the same evening, partook of an excellent supper at the hall situate at Mill House, where everything was served up in excellent style. A band of music was in attendance, and the evening was spent in the most agreeable manner. The arrangements made for the festivities, and the manner in which the whole was conducted, seems to give universal satisfaction to the workmen, for whom the "good cheer" was prepared."[2]_

One is left wondering what the boiler was used for normally!

Did love or affection play any part in the plans for marriage? If we believe the romantic tale then Thomas fell in love with Ellen at William Wakefield's hearing at the Rams Head in Disley. It would be pleasing to think that Ellen had found romance, but would it be likely?

Right through our tale Ellen had been a pawn. Wakefield's offence was seen to be against William Turner and his fortune, the

---

[2] The "Blackburn Mail" 16 / 1 / 1828

offence against Ellen herself was an important, but definitely a secondary, consideration.

Then, if we turn to the relationship between Turner and Thomas Legh in the next few years, it becomes obvious that Turner became involved in Thomas' businesses in Newton as did Henry Critchley, Ellen's uncle, though to a lesser extent. The date of the first meeting between Thomas Legh and William Turner is unknown. Was it, perhaps, before Turner bought Shrigley? Did Legh know Critchley before he knew Turner? There are many unanswered questions, but it is possible that the marriage was planned before the abduction as a way of joining the two families' fortunes. Even if the marriage was a love match, the families became very much a business partnership.

Much remains to be discovered about Ellen and Thomas' life together. From the mid-nineteenth century onward, the Legh papers, now preserved at Greater Manchester County Record Office, are a marvellous record of everyday life, no bill seems ever to have been discarded whether it was for mending the children's trousers or for an important piece of statuary. But for the early part of that century the records are virtually non-existent. What little is known has usually been found as a small item in another archive which, on first inspection, has nothing whatever to do with Lyme or the Leghs.

From items in the press it is obvious that they partook fully in the social round. Their names appear in the lists of people visiting Buxton during the season and they acted as patrons of the fund-raising balls for local charities. The Stockport papers reported for weeks on the preparations for a fancy dress ball to raise money for the building of the Infirmary. At Miss Young's premises in the town, a Mr Cash from Liverpool hired or sold his collection of five hundred costumes to ticket holders. The ball went on until four in the morning. It raised over £300 for the building works. Future generations of the Leghs continued to support the Infirmary from the proceeds of the plays they performed during the Christmas and New Year festivities at Lyme.

Thomas was an M.P. and belonged to societies in London He was one of the founders of the Travellers' Club and the couple would have spent some time in London. But, like his father-in-law, he was a business man and his businesses were centred around the estate office in Newton le Willows. At this stage of his life he seems to have played an active part in the running of his concerns there.

Newton Races, 1831

Newton was ideally placed to benefit from the industrial revolution. Thomas' estate lay on vast coal seams which had been mined for many years. He saw huge benefits from the use of steam power in his mines and also in the use of railways to transport his coal. Newton was on the Liverpool Manchester railway line and he was one of only a very few landowners to welcome it onto his land. One of the line's features is the Sankey Viaduct, called Nine Arches by the people of Newton. On its completion Thomas and Ellen became the first members of the public to cross it. They were in a cart driven by a very young boy called William Hall, whose normal load was builders' debris.[3]

Perhaps Ellen accompanied her husband to Newton races. Certainly her father was a steward there. Prints exist of one of the meetings showing Thomas' newly built grandstand with all the fun of the fair going on in the background, just like the Derby meeting today. In the foreground are Thomas and William Turner with others on horseback but annoyingly, for this is the only depiction of William Turner so far found, it is not clear which gentleman is which.

Lyme was not neglected. Thomas was very interested in agricultural techniques and made many alterations in the way the Park was managed. Just before Christmas 1828 a bullock, one of Lyme's white cattle which the "Stockport Advertiser" described as being then nearly extinct, was killed. It weighed fifty scores and was twelve years old. Thomas sent a round of the meat to the King as a Christmas present.[4]

What is certain is that Ellen went through three pregnancies. The first resulted in the birth of a still born son at the start of November 1828. This was not an uncommon occurrence so there would have been no cause for undue concern though it must have meant a great deal of sorrow in both families. Then in February 1830 Ellen gave birth at Lyme to a daughter, Ellen Jane Legh. The mother was only just nineteen, there was every hope that in time she would produce a son.

Tragically it was not to be. In January, 1831 Ellen went into labour at a house in Berkeley Square in London. Both she and the child, the son for whom both families were waiting, died. It was just four

---

[3] "Notes relating to the history of Newton le Willows" C. Cole. 1937

[4] "Stockport Advertiser" 3 / 1 / 1829

weeks before her twentieth birthday and little Ellen Jane was not yet a year old.

One can only try to imagine the desolation of the Turners and Thomas. Ellen, a young girl of fifteen, had been abducted. It had taken two years of court hearings and public interest in their affairs before she was free of Wakefield. Then after three years of marriage Ellen's short life had cruelly cut short.

Her funeral was a grand affair. On Thursday, 27th January there was a breakfast for the 110 tenants of the Leghs in the Horse and Jockey[5] at Newton. Then in twos and on horseback, wearing hatbands and gloves presented to them for the occasion, they led the procession. After the tenants came six plumed mules which preceded the hearse drawn by six black horses. There were twelve carriages belonging to the family and dignitaries from the area. They were followed by two chaises and eight gigs. The coffin, covered in crimson velvet, was carried into St Oswald's church at Winwick by six clergymen. The service was conducted by the curate, the Rev. T Hinde.

Ellen's remains were then buried in the Legh vault. The sculpture commissioned to commemorate her life and death can still be seen in the Legh chapel at St Oswald's. On it is carved,

"IN THE VAULT OF THIS CHAPEL
ARE DEPOSITED THE REMAINS OF
ELLEN
THE DEARLY BELOVED
AND MOST DEEPLY LAMENTED WIFE
OF THOMAS LEGH ESQ
OF LYME HALL CHESHIRE
AND DAUGHTER OF
WILLIAM TURNER ESQ
OF SHRIGLEY PARK
IN THE SAME COUNTY
BORN 12TH FEBRUARY 1811
DIED 17TH JANUARY 1831
LEAVING AN ONLY SURVIVING CHILD
ELLEN JANE LEGH
BORN 1OTH FEBRUARY 1830"

[5] Now the Kirkfield Hotel opposite the church.

Ellen's Memorial in St Oswald's Church, Winwick

Life goes on

Ellen's life had been tragically short, her parents and her husband were still living and she had one surviving child, Ellen Jane. All the hopes that had been pinned on Ellen now were focused on this toddler. She could not inherit her father's vast estates, for those were entailed in the male line. But she was the heir to the Turner estate and fortune. Now she would have to be groomed to make a suitable marriage in the hope that she would produce a son.

William Turner continued his involvement with businesses on the Legh estates in South Lancashire. He went into partnership with Richard Evans and they began to lease many of Thomas Legh's concerns there, including mines and factories. But he was still involved with the calico printing factory in Blackburn. Both Jane and William took an interest in the town's affairs. Jane founded the almshouses at Bank Top which bear the Turner coat of arms. William was one of Blackburn's first MPs and caused great offence to some of the townsfolk, when his election address consisted of donating a barrel of beer to the voters, who broke it open in the churchyard. Jane Turner died in 1841, her husband in 1842 and they are buried in a vault in St John's churchyard in Blackburn.

After their deaths trustees looked after Shrigley on the behalf of little Ellen Jane to whom we will return shortly.

William's brother-in-law, Henry Critchley, had lived in Macclesfield, but he too was to become involved on the Legh estates around Newton. He put money into Turner's ventures there, though he did not take an active part in running them. He and his wife, Ellen, William's sister, ended their lives living at The Heyes, a house in Haydock. They are buried in St Peter's churchyard in Newton.

And what of Thomas? He had been a moving force behind the development of old and new industrial concerns, particularly related to mining and railways around Newton. But around the time of Ellen's death he began leasing them out to be managed by others like Turner and Evans. This brought in enormous sums to the Legh estates[1] enabling him to fund other schemes to develop housing and amenities in the area for rich industrialists from Manchester and Liverpool.

He took a great interest in the latest ideas in agriculture, carrying out huge drainage projects on the Lyme farms and in the Park itself. He never lost his interest in railways. One of his last projects was to promote the Stockport to Whaley Bridge line which then ran just outside the Park.

He remained a widower until 1843 when he married Maud Lowther. Maud had a large number of brothers and sisters and in 1845 Thomas appointed one of them, Brabazon as vicar at Disley. The following year Brabazon married sixteen year old Ellen Jane Legh and so Mr and Mrs Lowther came to own Shrigley Park. Mrs Lowther, Ellen's daughter, died in 1906 and it was her descendant who sold it to the Salesian Order in 1929. They built the adjacent chapel and converted the Hall into a residential college for two hundred boys training to become missionaries. It was sold in the 1980s and became an hotel. Shrigley Hall Hotel, Golf and Country Club is now part of the Paramount Hotel group.

Thomas died in 1857 and is buried in the churchyard at Disley. At the Rams Head a few months later in a grand ceremony, Maud opened the Stockport to Whaley Bridge line. The line was extended to Buxton and now the trains travel between Buxton and Blackpool. Thomas and Maud had no children, so Lyme and all the Legh estates were inherited by a nephew, William John Legh who took the title Newton when he received a peerage in 1892.

The Rams Head, where first William and then Edward Gibbon Wakefield were tried, was altered a few years later, but still serves travellers on the busy A6 through Disley.

The Wakefields were released in May 1830. William remained in his elder brother's shadow but eventually joined the army. He died in 1848. As for the dastardly Edward Gibbon Wakefield he continued his extraordinary life. Nina and Jerningham, his children, received the rest of their education from him each day in his prison cell. His descendant,

---

[1] "The Leghs and Haydock Coal" Geoff Simm. 2001

Col. Lowther with his mother, Ellen's daughter.
(Are the gentlemen on the right also her sons?)
Reproduced with permission from a photograph at Shrigley Hall Hotel

Irma O'Connor's account of his life, and theirs, in Newgate is based on family letters and diaries and makes fascinating reading.

As a convicted criminal, a political career in England for Wakefield was not feasible, but the colonies were a different matter. Before he was released he had published two pamphlets, one on his proposals for colonizing Australasia, the other entitled "A Letter from Sydney". Thus, from Newgate, he established himself as an expert on the colonies.

For the first few years after his release he took an interest in affairs at home, such as the plight of agricultural labourers, but he never deserted his theories on the colonies and in 1834 the South Australian Association was formed. In 1836 he gave evidence to a committee of the House of Commons which led to the founding of the New Zealand Society.

When Lord Durham was appointed Governor-General and Lord High Commissioner of Canada, he wanted to take Wakefield but, to avoid dissatisfaction and embarrassment, the government would only allow an unofficial appointment. When Durham's report on Canada was issued, it was said that Wakefield had had the ideas, they had been written down by Buller, the chief secretary, and Durham had signed it. It was certainly Wakefield who forced the government to publish the report by giving it to "The Times". In the 1840s Wakefield became an elected member of Lower Canada's House of Assembly. But he returned to England in 1844.

He then concentrated on New Zealand and emigrated there in 1852, sleeping in a specially made bed to avoid sea-sickness on the voyage! His reputation and ideas had preceded him and he had to resort to press articles to win the population round to his ideas. Six months later he was elected to the General Assembly. By 1854 his health had broken down and he spent the next few years living in seclusion. When he died in 1862 he left just £500. A portrait of him looking every inch the elder statesman hangs in Christchurch, New Zealand.

He had a loyal following and some years after his death his friends subscribed to a bust which was to commemorate his "statesmanlike qualities and disinterested efforts for the improvement of the Empire". It was presented to the Colonial Office in 1875.

His lengthy obituary in the "Gentleman's Magazine" quotes from the "Daily Telegraph's" glowing account of his later life,

"there is no part of the British Empire which does not feel in the actual circumstances of the day the effect of Edward Gibbon Wakefield's labours as a practical statesman; and perhaps the same tangible results in administrative and constructive reform can scarcely be traced to the single hand of any one other man during his own lifetime."[2]

Thus the villain of our tale is still remembered, has had books written on his life and had his bust placed in a government office, whilst Ellen, his innocent victim, is largely forgotten and disregarded.

What would the crowds, who hissed Wakefield when he was taken in custody from the Lords back to Newgate, have thought of this strange turn of events?

---

[2] "The Gentleman's Magazine" Vol CCX111 October, 1862